Kate Bruce is Deputy Warden and Tutor in Homiletics at Cranmer Hall, Durham. She is also Fellow in Preaching at CODEC (<www.dur.ac.uk/codec/>) a research centre focusing on engaging faith in digital culture. Kate runs the Durham Preaching Conference and teaches preaching around the UK, working with clergy, Readers and young preachers. She is an experienced and sought-after preacher. Her published works include Lent courses: *Life Source* (2006), *Life Calling* (2007), co-authored with Robert Warren, and *Igniting the Heart: Preaching and imagination* (2015). She is particularly interested in the relationship between preaching and stand-up comedy, and performs stand-up as 'Woman of the Cloth'.

Jamie Harrison is a Reader at St Nicholas Durham, Chair of the House of Laity in the Church of England's General Synod, and a member of the Clergy Discipline Commission. A former GP Adviser to the Department of Health, he is Fellow in Healthcare and Religion at St John's College, Durham University. He has published widely on issues of vocation (Grove Monograph), medical careers and the NHS, receiving the Baxter Award from the European Health Management Association in 2000 for *Clinical Governance in Primary Care*. With Bishop Robert Innes, he recently edited the book *Clergy in a Complex Age: Responses to the Guidelines for the professional conduct of the clergy* (SPCK, 2016).

WRESTLING WITH THE WORD

Preaching tricky texts

Edited by Kate Bruce and
Jamie Harrison

First published in Great Britain in 2016

Society for Promoting Christian Knowledge
36 Causton Street
London SW1P 4ST
www.spck.org.uk

British Library Cataloguing-in-Publication Data
A catalogue record for this book is available from the British Library

ISBN 978–0–281–07648–2
eBook ISBN 978–0–281–07649–9

Typeset by Graphicraft Limited, Hong Kong
First printed in Great Britain by Ashford Press Ltd
Subsequently digitally printed in Great Britain

eBook by Graphicraft Limited, Hong Kong

Produced on paper from sustainable forests

This book is dedicated to David Day
(born 11 August 1936)
and to the Readers of the Church of England,
who celebrate their 150th anniversary in 2016

Contents

———•◦•———

Part 1
THEOLOGICAL FOUNDATIONS

Part 2
SERMONS ON TRICKY TEXTS

Contents

Part 3
WRESTLING WITH THE WORD

Contributors

John Bell is a member of the Iona Community.

Richard Briggs is Lecturer in Old Testament and Director of Biblical Studies at Cranmer Hall, Durham.

Kate Bruce is Deputy Warden and Tutor in Homiletics at Cranmer Hall, Durham.

David Day is a former Principal of St John's College, Durham.

James Dunn is Emeritus Lightfoot Professor of Divinity at Durham University.

Ruth Etchells (1931–2012) was Principal of St John's College, Durham, 1979–88.

Lis Goddard is Vicar of St James the Less Westminster.

Lindsey Goodhew is Honorary Curate of St Nicholas Durham.

Jamie Harrison is a Reader at St Nicholas Durham.

Jolyon Mitchell has a personal Chair in Communication, Arts and Religion at Edinburgh University.

Walter Moberly is Professor of Theology and Biblical Interpretation at Durham University.

John Pritchard is a former Bishop of Oxford.

Roy Searle is one of the leaders of the Northumbria Community.

Magdalen Smith is Director of Ordinands for Chester Diocese.

Geoffrey Stevenson is an Honorary Fellow at the School of Divinity, Edinburgh University.

Miriam Swaffield is the Student Mission Leader for Fusion and a postgraduate at Cranmer Hall, Durham.

Mark Tanner is Bishop of Berwick.

Justin Welby is Archbishop of Canterbury.

Alison Wilkinson is a Methodist minister in Newcastle.

David Wilkinson is Principal of St John's College, Durham.

Foreword

It's fashionable to say that preaching is going out of fashion. The era of public lectures or long speeches at political rallies is past, they say. Listen to the 2-minute, 45-second pieces on the *Today* programme on Radio 4. If you can't say it in two sentences you'll be interrupted; if you try to develop an argument you'll be cut off. Social media is where the action is and the idea of a 10-, 20- or even 30-minute monologue is simply impossible, 'so last century'. That is, until you hear a really good preacher.

There's a story (probably apocryphal) about the sceptical eighteenth-century philosopher David Hume hurrying down a road when he's met by a friend. 'Can't stop,' says Hume, 'I'm off to hear George Whitfield preach.' 'But you don't believe a word of it,' replied his friend in astonishment. 'No,' came the response, 'but Whitfield does.'

When a preacher speaks with passion about matters of burning importance and genuine personal significance, the preacher will get a hearing in any age. Indeed, there are few times and places in society now where listeners are lifted up and reminded of their capacity for the infinite, and a well-constructed and well-delivered sermon has the potential to inspire people as few other experiences can.

Nevertheless, preachers can be undermined by the current scepticism both about sermons and about their subject, the good news about God. If preachers get to the stage where they feel they have to say something, rather than that they have something to say, a rather critical line has been crossed. Or if the preacher seems to be a mild-mannered person speaking to mild-mannered people in a mild-mannered way about mild-mannered things it won't be surprising if the congregation focus on the number of panes in the east window or the number of shopping days to Christmas. It's not just Whitfield who needed to feel passionate about what he had to say; all of us called to preach in any age need to feel the same. These are wonderful and weighty matters of which we speak and I have long treasured the words attributed to Thomas Carlyle: 'Who, having been called to be a preacher, would stoop to be a king?'

The corollary, however, is that preaching is a tough task. It won't do to wander into the pulpit simply saying the Holy Spirit will inspire us. As every first-time preacher discovers, the Holy Spirit is a joint partner in this start-up company; we both have to work at it. We need to ask very basic questions, like: What is our sermon for? What is it trying to say? (If we can't summarize the message in two sentences at the top of the page it won't be surprising if our listeners can't do it either.) Who is it for, that is, what's the make-up of this congregation, on this day, in this context? We need to ask how it proposes to engage the congregation and what it is intended to do for them. A sermon isn't an exercise in intellectual bravado; it's not an essay, a lecture, an exhortation, a counselling session, a testimony. It's a declaration of the good news for these good people at this particular time and place. It's summed up for me in the prayer with which I usually open a sermon: 'Gracious God, may these *spoken* words be faithful to the *written* words and lead us to the *living* Word, Jesus Christ our Lord, Amen.'

A tough task, perhaps, but a glorious and fascinating one.

Because preaching is such a privilege, churches take seriously who they ask to do it. In the Church of England preaching is one of the key responsibilities of Readers, or Licensed Lay Ministers (LLMs), and they have a three-year training so that they have the knowledge, understanding and wisdom to equip them for both this and their other opportunities for ministry. These are special people, and to be treasured. An American bishop once had a notice in his office that said, 'Your bishop needs to know he's loved; give him a hug.' Give your Readers and LLMs a hug too. They do wonderful work with great commitment and little enough thanks.

The Church of England has had Readers in its ranks now for 150 years. Like all preachers, Readers always want to make their sermons more effective, and seek help in the process of preparing and crafting sermons. I'm sure this book will soon be on the shelves of many Readers and LLMs, but also of clergy and lay preachers of many denominations, particularly because it focuses on preaching on those biblical texts that make the preacher's heart sink when he or she faces them. Occasions when you think it might have been helpful if Jesus had had a Communications Officer to advise him, or when you wish the Lord hadn't wanted to smite the Amalekites quite so enthusiastically. This book is full of wisdom on these tricky texts; I can almost hear the penny dropping with delight as people read these examples of preaching on hard passages.

One of the best preachers I have ever encountered on these or any texts is David Day, who is honoured in the compilation of the book. I worked with David for some years and have sat at his feet many times as he has unpicked the tangled threads of particular passages and made them shine with life and hope. His clear thinking and illuminating insights, shot through with contemporary images and delightful humour, have brought me and thousands of others both pleasure in the gospel and challenge in the gospel's demands. David's books on preaching have become standards; his training courses have been enormously popular, combining rigour and fun, but above all his preaching has been inspirational and caused many of us to return to the task with fresh enthusiasm.

Martin Luther, whose hammering of 95 theses on to a church door in Wittenberg in 1517 sparked the Reformation, was by reputation a powerful preacher. He once wrote this:

A good preacher should have these properties and virtues: First, he (*sic*) should be able to teach in a right and orderly way. Second, he should have a good wit. Third, he should be able to speak well. Fourth, he should have a good voice. Fifth, a good memory. Sixth, he should know when to stop. Seventh, he should make sure of his material and be diligent. Eighth, he should stake body and blood, goods and honour on it. Ninth, he must suffer himself to be vexed and flayed by everyone.

'Flayed by everyone'? We were doing so well! Misunderstood, perhaps. Not always as effective as we'd like to be. But striving to be better. Always striving to be better.

+John Pritchard

Preface

————•◆•————

This book is challenging. It challenged the editors in their editing and those commissioned to write sermons in their writing. It will challenge you, dear reader (Reader). It is meant to challenge.

But this book is also shaped to offer advice and encouragement. It gathers responses to uncomfortable passages found in Holy Scripture, and proffers renewed confidence in the Bible's power to speak into our contemporary world. It is meant to be helpful, but not to be comfortable.

This book exposes the twilight world of the book of Judges, pondering the murder of an unnamed innocent girl and that of a battle-weary general. It exposes the human heart to scrutiny and often comes away saddened, full of questions. How can one preach on a psalm that wants to shatter the heads of infants? And how does one make sense of the spiteful beheading of a man whose only mistake was to complain about a woman's marital status, or seemingly harsh words about divorce, or of the need to obey the government of the day whatever?

Yet this book is full of hope. There is the hope of eternal life in Jesus Christ, and of belief in a God who created, and continues to do so. There are pictures of worship and praise that seek to bring others into God's presence. There is the hope that apparently harsh words on the place of women in the Church can be morphed into something joyful and precious. And all the time, God is seeking to break through the text to say, 'I am with you and won't let you go.'

So who is this book for?

This book is for those who preach and those who hear preachers. It offers advice on the shape and structure of sermons, and how to navigate the stormy waters of tricky texts. It says 'Don't avoid them!' and 'Please don't develop your own little set of comfortable passages, your "canon within a canon", where you feel at ease.' Given the choice from two or three set readings for the day, be willing to take on the taxing one. And where you are going through a Bible book, resist the temptation to miss out the difficult verse or two, even if the lectionary does. Resist such temptation and be brave!

This book is for readers of the Bible, those who read but would prefer to pass over the doubtful and divisive texts that seem to have no place in Holy Scripture. To you we send an urgent plea – stay with the text and see if anything in this book can encourage you and give you more hope than you thought possible. We start each chapter with a prayer, realizing that even if we are right in what we think about a given text, you may not agree, and we need to pray for God's ongoing help in the matter.

How is the book shaped?

This book is in three parts. After some introductory comments, we offer two chapters wrestling with the arguments against preaching, and fleshing out theological foundations that undergird the principles of how to preach on tricky texts. There then follows a series of chapters – sermons, themed in sets of three: texts beyond human experience, of violence, terror, strangeness and abrasion. Each set of sermons is prefaced by a brief introduction and ends with comment on some of the homiletic strategies employed. The third part looks at how ancient words can apply to contemporary contexts.

Three other sermons

Three other, publicly preached, sermons populate the book. The first is by David Day, once a Reader in the Church of England and now a self-supporting priest. We reproduce a sermon he gave at the annual Durham Diocesan Readers' service in Durham Cathedral on 19 September 2015. This book is dedicated to David, as he celebrates his eightieth birthday, along with all Readers, as they rejoice in 150 years of ministry in the Church of England. So we give thanks to God for such ministries, praying for their continued flourishing.

A second sermon was preached by Justin Welby, Archbishop of Canterbury, on Ascension Day 2015. It shows how tricky texts can overlap with tricky subjects, as he grapples with the first 11 verses of Acts chapter 1. How easy for our minds to wander to famous oil paintings of feet, disappearing skywards, and miss the deeper, challenging call to follow a risen and now ascended Lord. Here is a sermon to ponder, with its call to action, not just contemplation.

The third, additional, sermon was the last one preached by the late Ruth Etchells, former Principal of St John's College, Durham, lay theologian, scholar, spiritual director, friend and inspiration to many. Ruth does her usual trick of quoting widely and wonderfully from a range of authors and poets (and so causing the editors grief over matters of copyright!), showing us the power of such texts to enlarge our imaginations and broaden our horizons. Two poems – 'Song' (by Veronica Zundel) and 'The Last Enemy' (by Stewart Henderson) – are published, with permission and in full, as part of the book.

Your challenge

So the challenge is now yours. Our prayer, trust and belief is that you can and will rise to it, more able and more confident when next you face a 'tricky text'.

Kate Bruce and Jamie Harrison

A Readers' sermon: Isaiah 40.1–8

DAVID DAY

'Comfort, O comfort my people, says your God . . .
A voice says "Cry out!" and I said, "What shall I cry?"'
(Isaiah 40.1, 6a)

It's a great thing to welcome new Readers. Readers are lay people, from all walks of life, called by God, and licensed by the Church to preach, teach, lead worship and assist in pastoral, evangelistic and liturgical work. At least, that's what it says on the Readers' website. There are now over 10,000 Readers. And in July 2016 we celebrated 150 years of Reader ministry.

But what do they do? Well . . . first in the list is that they preach. Oh dear. I wonder what came into your mind when I said that. Mark Twain once said, 'If all the people who listen to sermons every Sunday were laid end to end, they would all be much more comfortable.' Preaching doesn't have a great reputation. Over two hundred years ago a little boy said to his mother, 'Oh pay the man, mother, and let us go home.' Walter Burghardt wrote in a book for preachers: 'Assume they would rather feed their children to crocodiles than listen to you.' None of this is encouraging.

Our Old Testament reading plunges us into the heart of Reader ministry. 'A voice says, "Cry out!" And I said, "What shall I cry?"' It sounds like a Reader on a Saturday night. 'I have nothing to say tomorrow morning. Only 12 hours to go. I've got two terrible jokes and a calendar motto. What am I to do?' The voice says again, 'Cry.' It is not the ghost of the vicar speaking. The command comes from the throne of God. The Reader replies, 'Give me some help here, Lord. What shall I cry?' And he or she gets an answer. 'All people are grass, their constancy is like the flower of the field. The grass withers, the flower fades . . . surely the people are grass.'

Oh boy, that will really go down well. I can hear Colonel Fortescue complaining now. But let's take it seriously. What *are* we to cry? I want to re-jig the reading from Isaiah.

The Reader's job is quite simple. Two tasks.

Task one: put into words what people know in their hearts.

Beneath the surface – even beneath the surface of the confident, together people, the efficient, golden men and women who've got it all, there's often a deep dissatisfaction. People know that something is wrong. They're not winning. They long for a different life. Freddie Mercury said, 'You can have everything in the world and still be the loneliest man.' Prince Charles said, 'There remains deep in the soul a persistent anxiety that something is missing.' Ian Hislop said, 'I'm desperate but not admitting it. I keep wanting.'

The preacher puts into words what people know in their hearts. I remember two women who came to our church. They were walking along the beach at Roker. One said to the other, 'There's got to be more to life than this.' They decided to give church a go.

What shall I cry? 'Nothing lasts.' An odd piece of good news. Nothing lasts – not the car bodywork; not the stone work on the east end of the cathedral; not state-of-the-art computers. The preacher's job is to put into words what people feel deep down in their hearts. So that what follows is what's been called 'the nod of recognition'. *Yeah, that is what it's like. That's exactly what I feel.*

I remember when I was teaching in a secondary school. One morning the Biology teacher exploded into the staff room at break. 'What's up?' I asked. 'Bad morning!' he replied. It transpired that he'd been teaching the life cycle of the frog. You know – those little pictures of frogspawn, tadpoles, tadpoles with wings, ending up with a picture of a frog. (You can tell I wasn't great at Biology.) One pupil found the process difficult. 'What's it all about, sir?' she wailed. 'It just goes round and round. What's it all about?' I was intrigued. 'What did you say?' I asked. He replied, 'Get it down

in your book and colour it in or you'll stay in at break.' Years later
I still think the pupil was right and the teacher was wrong.

We are restless creatures, haunted by the question, 'Can I find love
and happiness and security in a world that often lets me down?'
St Augustine wrote, 'You have made us for Yourself, O Lord, and
our hearts are restless until they find their rest in You.' Milton
Jones says, 'It's like trying to hear a SatNav that you've locked
in the boot of the car because you thought you wouldn't need it.'

Readers have two tasks. The first is – you put into words what
people know in their hearts.

Task Two: put into words what God feels in his heart.

People think God is soft and soppy like Father Christmas. Or
he is actually rather nasty – causing tsunamis and cancer. God
says, 'Tell them what I'm like.' Put into words the pain, love, longing of the Living God, who is desperate to make all things new.
Let people hear *in us* the urgency of God pleading that people
might come to know him and that Christians might show his
love in their lives. Milton Jones again: 'God is like Mozart, and we
are the notes. God is the AA, and we are the breakdowns. God is
Calvin Klein. We are pants.'

Help people to see Jesus afresh. The Jesus who sees the woman
desperately trying to make ends meet when the electricity bill
arrives, and knows she is harassed. The Jesus who sees the man
made redundant in his fifties, and knows he is helpless. The Jesus
who sees the youth throwing his lager can out of the car, and
sees that he is a sheep without a shepherd. The Jesus who knows
about worries over children, over money, finding real love, getting
some space in which to live. The Jesus who knows about the desire
to start again, the need for forgiveness and the God-shaped ache
in the heart. The Jesus who heals the broken-hearted and brings
new life to the dead.

The word of our God stands for ever. A Reader told me how
exhilarating it was to meet someone who said, 'I came to faith
through a sermon you preached thirty years ago.' Weak words, but

brought to life by the Spirit's breath. The word of our God stands for ever.

You put into words what God feels in his heart. Tell them, as our reading does, that God is on the move. Bear witness to a God who is like a mountain stream that can never be stopped. 'The grass withers, the flower fades; but the word of our God will stand for ever.' 'Make straight in the desert a highway for our God.' Put into words what God feels in his heart.

Thomas Carlyle reputedly asked, 'Who, having been called to be a preacher, would stoop to be a king?' Or a queen. A Reader's main job is to preach. What a privilege.

How can we support these new Readers? How can we support all those Readers who faithfully try to speak the word of the Lord in our churches?

1 Before the sermon: pray for them. Talk to them about the sermon. Ask if you can help with illustrations and examples and stories from your experience. One human being cannot think up a dozen illustrations; their imaginations will run dry. Preparing a sermon is a lonely business. Preachers need you to prepare with them.
2 During the sermon: listen carefully. Look interested. Give them eye contact. Never, ever, shut your eyes. They will not think you are praying or meditating. They will think you are asleep.
3 After the sermon: talk to them. Say what you found helpful. Mention what you found unusual or surprising. Gently, oh so gently, ask probing questions. 'What were you trying to say when you compared the Church to apple crumble?' This is more encouraging than, 'You got it down to six minutes today.' 'Couldn't hear a word you said.' Or, 'Did you know there are 249 panes of glass in the east window?'

It's been said: 'Congregations get the preachers they deserve.' Ouch. But there's a truth there. We, as the body of Christ, have a responsibility to engage, enliven, enable, energize and to encourage those who bring us the word of God. Amen.

Part 1

THEOLOGICAL FOUNDATIONS

1

The call to preach

KATE BRUCE

Do you ever find yourself doing the rounds with a spectacularly tricky text and thinking, 'What am I doing?' Do you spend hours pondering, praying, researching and writing, and then wonder: will this sermon make any difference to anything? Is it self-indulgent? What right do I have to speak to these people? In a context where there are voices claiming that the day of the sermon is over,[1] the preacher needs to think through: what is preaching, and what's the point?

Before we go any further I sense an elephant perched on the coffee table; an elephant we need to name. The negative connotations of the word 'preach' in everyday parlance hardly give it a ringing endorsement. It is easy to caricature preaching as declamatory, one-way, authoritarian, pontificating pulpit patter of the 'should' and 'ought' variety. Is it just an expression of old-school paternalism, which treats people like empty vessels longing to be filled up with useful information about the fate, for example, of the Jebusites? Many of us have experienced flesh on this particular straw man; caricature can come horribly close to experience. So, shouldn't we just cease the practice and be done with it?

---

[1] See, for example: Norrington, D. C., *To Preach or Not to Preach*. Paternoster Press, Carlisle, 1996; Murray, S., *Post-Christendom, Church and Mission in a Strange New World*. Paternoster Press, Carlisle, 2004; Pagitt, D., *Preaching Re-imagined: The Role of the Sermon in Communities of Faith*. Zondervan, Grand Rapids, MI, 2005; Baker, J., *Transforming Preaching: Communicating God's Word in a Postmodern World*. Grove Books, Cambridge, 2009.

Preaching: wrestling with understanding

Before we discard preaching, it would be wise to understand what we would be losing. Looking at six of the more common verbs used in the New Testament for preaching gives us a sense of its scope. *Martyrein* means to witness; *parakalein* to comfort or admonish; *propheteuein* means to prophesy; and *didaskein* refers to teaching. *Keryssein*, meaning to proclaim, is very close to *euangelizesthai* or preach the good news.[2] This is not simply proclamation of an event in the past but of the presence of Christ now, inaugurating a new apprehension of reality.

A key question for any preacher is, 'What am I trying to do in this sermon?' A sermon may proclaim, involving witness and elements of admonition or comfort. It may invite consideration of the gospel, as with the more direct evangelistic address. It will always seek to identify something of the presence of God in the given moment and thus have a prophetic edge. While there are often aspects of teaching in the sermon, it is always more than a teaching event. The sermon alone simply cannot be expected to develop the biblical literacy of the congregation; this belongs to the wider teaching ministry of the Church.

In summary: the sermon is an event in which by the grace of God and in the power of the Holy Spirit, Christ is present. There is clearly here an argument for the sermon as sacramental event.[3] Preaching is more than an appeal to cognition: it is a corporate event in time that seeks to ignite the heart, appeal to the mind, and move the will.

Preaching: wrestling with the objections

Let's attend more closely to that elephant perched on the coffee table and wrestle with the criticisms that have been levelled at preaching.

---

[2] Runia, K., *The Sermon Under Attack*. Paternoster Press, Exeter, 1983, pp. 20, 26.
[3] Bruce, K., *Igniting the Heart: Preaching and Imagination*. SCM Press, London, 2015, pp. 85–106.

Under the oppressive boot?

Doug Pagitt sees preaching in terms of 'speaching'; an authoritarian practice with the preacher as 'teller'.[4] Similarly, Stuart Murray denounces preaching as 'declaiming from an authoritarian height', a vestige of Christendom, 'related to clericalism, massive buildings, unchallengeable proclamation and nominal congregations'.[5] Implicit in these critiques is a failure to differentiate between *authoritarian* and *authoritative* preaching. Preaching as an *authoritarian*, controlling practice can have no place in the Church; bullying, declamatory certitude lacks love, imagination and wisdom. Honesty, openness and vulnerability, undergirded by love for the hearer, are hallmarks of the *authoritative* preacher.

Honesty means not glossing over the difficulties in the Scriptures; we cannot pretend that tricky, thorny texts do not exist. Ignoring them will lead to preaching a very selective canon and sliding over challenging material. Sometimes the Bible does not seem to contain good news for many of its characters. This needs to be wrestled with, to see how such texts might be handled responsibly.

The preacher is first audience of the sermon. Nadia Bolz-Weber, a Lutheran pastor in the USA, asked her congregation for feedback on her preaching: 'Almost all of them said that they love that their preacher is so obviously preaching to herself and just allowing them to overhear it.'[6] Her authority as a preacher comes from her honest struggle to live authentically; she inhabits her sermons. In contrast, Frederick Buechner critiques a form of preaching in which 'men in business suits get up and proclaim the faith with the dynamic persuasiveness of insurance salesmen . . . you feel there is no mystery that has not been solved, no secrets there that can escape detection'.[7]

---

[4] Pagitt, *Preaching Re-imagined*, pp. 21–32.
[5] Murray, *Post-Christendom: Church and Mission in a Strange New World*, p. 230.
[6] Bolz-Weber, N., *Accidental Saints: Finding God in All the Wrong People*. Canterbury Press, Norwich, 2015, p. 30.
[7] Buechner, F., *Telling Secrets*. HarperOne, New York, 1991, p. 84.

There can be an unimaginative, rabid certainty in preaching, deeply off-putting in a culture more open to the nudge of suggestion. Buechner describes another kind of preaching that is 'not seamless and armor plated'.[8] Such preaching is deeply and deliberately earthed in the life of the preacher: it is authentic, open and honest.

Challenging, provocative sermons that boldly ask us to wrestle with tricky texts and to be honest about our conflicted lives are part of the formation of a mature community, a means of drawing people in and deepening faith.[9] There is a place for authoritative monologue in homiletics, but there is no place for authoritarian hectoring that seeks to enforce conformity and crush dissent.

Generates passive hearers?

Listening to a sermon can become a passive exercise if the content and performance fail to engage, and if the hearers do not regard themselves as in part responsible for the making of the sermon. Attentive listening involves concentration, analysis and question. The sermon we hear will never be quite the same as the sermon preached, since the active listener is working on the interface between the words spoken and their own particular situation and experience. 'It is the sermons we preach to ourselves around the preacher's sermons that are the ones we hear most powerfully.'[10]

The preacher's challenge is to engage active listening. This calls, among other things, for preachers to name difficulties with tricky texts, bringing the congregation with them in the journey. This is a matter of courageous questioning, compelling content

---

[8] Buechner, *Telling Secrets*, p. 84.
[9] Northcutt, K. L., *Kindling Desire for God: Preaching as Spiritual Direction*. Fortress Press, Minneapolis, MN, 2009.
[10] Buechner, *Telling Secrets*, p. 85.

and creative performance. In this view the work of the preacher is close to that of an artist, a poet or a linguistic musician. Sitting and listening does not have to mean passivity. Murray, although opposed to monologue preaching, writes of the importance of poets and storytellers stirring the churches into re-imagining God's kingdom.[11] Storytellers deliver monologues but we don't connect listening to their speech with passivity. Walter Brueggemann argues for preaching to be seen as poetic speech that peels back the layers of inanity and tedium and discloses new hope and new possibility.[12] The genuine reception of such disclosure is far from passive. A number of theological questions fall out from this. Who makes the sermon? Is it God, the preacher's skill or the listeners' attentiveness? What is the theological importance of deep listening? (See Chapter 2).

Poor means of teaching?

Some argue that preaching is an ineffective means of teaching, creating a dependency on the preacher, who is seen as an expert among those largely ignorant of faith.[13] But what is meant by 'teaching'? The communication of information relating to Christian belief and practice is only one aspect of preaching. The sermon is a form of discourse that seeks to engage hearts as well as minds; an invitational exploration of a text and its implications in a particular context. It is part of the sacramental life of the Church and feeds into the Church's wider teaching ministry.

'The sermon fails to develop powers of thought and analytical skills.'[14] This might be a valid objection if the sermon does not pose sharp questions, drawing in congregational engagement, perhaps through naming problems in the text and inviting the

---

[11] Murray, *Post-Christendom: Church and Mission in a Strange New World*, pp. 277, 283.

[12] Brueggemann, W., *Finally Comes the Poet: Daring Speech for Proclamation*. Fortress Press, Minneapolis, MN, 1989, pp. 1–11.

[13] Norrington, *To Preach or Not to Preach*, p. 76.

[14] Norrington, *To Preach or Not to Preach*, p. 77.

congregation to join in wrestling with such challenges. A sermon that facilitates congregational application, opening opportunities for further discussion, has the potential to draw congregations into deeper, critical biblical engagement.

Doug Pagitt argues that preaching 'takes the Bible away from the hearers . . . and reminds them that they are not in a position to speak on how they are implicated by this story'.[15] On the contrary, the preacher has the opportunity and responsibility to enthuse, challenge, and encourage the hearer. The preacher asks explicitly or implicitly, 'Where are you in this text?' 'How do you respond?' 'So what difference does this make to us?' The purpose of the sermon is not to dominate and disempower but to serve the community, inviting people to read and wrestle with the text for themselves.

The effective preacher comes alongside the hearers, asking difficult questions of the text, exploring possible responses, and provoking the hearer to think, question, dream and pray. If the sermon does lead to disengagement with the Scriptures perhaps the issue lies less with the practice of preaching and more with the approach of the specific preacher, the ethos of the community, and the nature of its leadership. The preacher is not the biblical gatekeeper. He or she is much closer to the co-pilgrim on the way who lifts our eyes to the horizon, names the struggle when the terrain is rough, and offers some map-reading suggestions as we journey in faith together.

Assumes same starting point for all?

The sermon is 'bound to fail because its regular use presupposes a similar starting point, learning ability, stage of faith and growth rate for *all* in the congregation *all* of the time'.[16] This criticism is aimed at the sermon that assumes that everyone begins at point

---

[15] Pagitt, *Preaching Re-imagined*, p. 31.
[16] Norrington, *To Preach or Not to Preach*, p. 76.

A and everyone will move to point B through the sermon. But, even in using this kind of logical structure, would it matter hugely if a hearer focused on one part and missed the rest? If we believe in a God who speaks into the specifics of people's lives then we would fully expect different people to hear different things in the sermon. The assumption of uniformity in the hearers and in what they might hear in the sermon suggests a weak theology of revelation (see Chapter 2).

We would not argue that a story, a picture or a piece of drama couldn't work with a mixed group. There are plenty of examples of films that can be read at different levels by adults and children. There is no reason why the sermon should not be accessible to more than one kind of learner or age group at the same time. In this sense the sermon is similar to a musical score; everyone needs to be able to discern the melodic line of the sermon, a melody that forms the main flow of the argument, or unfolding of the narrative. However, there should be plenty of opportunity for the listener to hear deeper resonances and harmonies through the preacher's use of image, instance, illustration and biblical allusion.

The hope is that in the sermon-event there will be a fusion of ideas and something new born in each hearer. An effective sermon is one that triggers new vision, a deeper experience of God, perhaps in the form of a new challenge that won't be silenced, or a deep sense of reassurance and peace.

Pastorally ineffective

It has been claimed that the monologue sermon creates impaired participation, resulting in personal problems not being addressed.[17] However, we cannot possibly expect the sermon to be the source of answers to the varied issues with which people struggle. Pastoral support might be offered and received through the sermon in a

---

[17] Norrington, *To Preach or Not to Preach*, p. 71.

general sense, and the preacher's own pastoral wisdom – for good or ill – will certainly be in evidence to the hearer, but any church functioning effectively will have a variety of sources of specific pastoral care.

Norrington argues that apathy results from the sermon when there is too great a focus on sinfulness and a lack of emphasis on grace.[18] He is quite right! Most of us already live with a sharp sense of our shortcomings and don't need to be reminded of our failures. The problem is not that I don't know I am sinful and foolish. It is that I don't seem to be able to dig myself out of the quicksand of my own making. There is no point telling me I *ought to do this* and I *should do that*. I know! I would if I could, but I can't. To borrow from St Paul, 'Who will rescue me from this body of death?' (Romans 7.24). Certainly not the preacher who comes to beat me up with the 'should' stick. However, one who reminds me of the grace of God in Christ, who encourages me to allow myself to be picked up and re-orientated to God; this is the preacher who helps me to see new possibilities, bringing hope and encouragement.

Not all preachers are good at it!

Effective preaching requires particular skills. There are innately good communicators, but preaching skills can always be improved, and preachers taught to hone their art. This raises the question of how preachers are selected and trained, and where they receive ongoing mentoring, not least in relation to Reader training in the Anglican Church. Given that Readers express so much of their ministry through preaching, access to high-quality initial training, followed by continuing ministerial education, not least in preaching, should be at least as comprehensive as that given to their ordained colleagues. This raises questions about parity across theological education institutions in the training of lay and

---

[18] Norrington, *To Preach or Not to Preach*, p. 78.

ordained preachers. Allied to this, across the denominations, how are younger preachers being identified and trained so that they are theologically thoughtful, reflective practitioners, rather than preachers who simply echo uncritically the models of preaching they observe?

The wise preacher will seek honest feedback from congregation members and from fellow preachers. However, many hearers find it difficult to give clear feedback; 'Nice sermon, Vicar' is not helpful! Training a small group of people in what to look for, and how to balance affirmation and constructive criticism, is enormously helpful for the preachers who want to evaluate their praxis. A video of the preacher in a live context allows the preacher to reach informed self-evaluation.

Performance: a dirty word?

Norrington argues dismissively that some people like sermons 'because they enjoy watching a good performance'.[19] Is such enjoyment merely a superficial matter, or is it a potential doorway into deeper engagement with God? In response to the concern that preaching is being dumbed down to something that is merely entertaining, we might observe that while entertainment can refer to something shallow and superficial it is also linked to hospitality. If you come to my home for a meal, I am 'entertaining' you, making space for you around my table. If you 'entertain' an idea you are giving consideration to it. Like 'performance', 'entertainment' doesn't have to be a dirty word.

Linked to this is the criticism that in our image-dominated society people can no longer concentrate for more than a few minutes. The reality is that people are perfectly capable of focusing and giving attention if they are engaged. If the sermon fails to achieve this the reason may be because the material and the delivery are not engaging. Performance matters!

---

[19] Norrington, *To Preach or Not to Preach*, p. 80.

Such criticisms call upon preachers to wrestle with their understanding of preaching. Preaching maintains a vital and honoured place within the life of the Church, something to be celebrated and not eliminated.

Questions to consider

- What do you think makes for an effective sermon?
- Do you agree with the arguments presented in response to the range of criticisms of the sermon? Would you challenge or develop them in any way?
- What sustains you as a preacher on those days when preparation is difficult and response a tad stony?

2

Wrestling with the theology of preaching

KATE BRUCE

A theology of preaching sustains and nourishes the pulpit with a constancy that survives the ebb and flow of the feelings of the one standing in it as well as the smiles and frowns of those who sit before it.[1]

Securely grasping the theological foundations of preaching gives a sense of security, especially when wrestling with tricky texts. Checking the lectionary readings and avoiding the thorny passages results in a preaching diet lacking the richness of scriptural variety. Non-lectionary users may be tempted to form a 'canon within the canon', rarely venturing into more challenging territory. There is danger in ruling some texts offside; it communicates implicitly the message that there are certain things God does not permit us to articulate and process. This leads to a silencing of question and of protest and a muting of doubt and failure: important aspects of a deepening life of faith. Nice, tame, lame preaching reflects a world none of us inhabits. Here is a plea for preaching that names hard truths and is prepared to wrestle, Jacob-like, through the night-time, seeking the blessing of God. Such preaching travels through shadowy places in search of genuine hope, without fleeing to the false lights of easy answers and cheap grace. Having a secure

---

[1] Craddock, F. B., *Preaching*. Abingdon, Nashville, TN, 1985, p. 48.

theology of preaching gives the preacher the courage to seek God in texts that look, at first glance, somewhat uncongenial.

Wrestling with tricky texts is demanding; the reward comes when the congregation leans in with the nod of recognition: 'I always wondered about that, but didn't think I could ask.' Such preaching offers hope that God is to be found in and through the struggle. It communicates to the listener that this preacher is not satisfied with easy slick answers, but searches for God in places that appear as arid and lifeless as the valley of dry bones. Such courageous preaching offers tangible hope precisely because it has journeyed through the byways of struggle. The difficulties of this are mitigated by grasping a clear theology of preaching; a compass in the fog. This logically begins with consideration of revelation, beginning with reflection on the nature of the God in whose name the preacher speaks.

The communicating God

Scripture reveals God as the great communicator. God speaks, and his words are powerful, effective and creative; the God who *speaks* is the God who *acts* through his words.[2] In Genesis 1, the creative power of God's word is demonstrated in the repeated phrase 'and God said'. His Word brings all aspects of creation into being; God speaks and it is so. Again and again God speaks in word and symbol, calling and empowering people to speak his message into their contexts. 'Human beings are constituted by God's words to live by God's words and to communicate by words.'[3]

When Moses attempts to dodge the divine call with numerous objections, God responds with many assurances, culminating with the pledge that he will help both Moses and Aaron to speak: 'You

---

[2] Adam, P., *Speaking God's Words: A Practical Theology of Preaching*. Regent College Publishing, Vancouver, BC, 1996, p. 15.
[3] Quicke, M. J., *360 Degree Preaching*. Baker Academic, Grand Rapids, MI, 2003, p. 55.

[Aaron] shall speak to him and put the words in his mouth; and I will be with your mouth and with his mouth, and will teach you what you shall do' (Exodus 4.15).

This theme of divine empowerment recurs in Isaiah 6. Faced with a vision of the holiness of God, Isaiah is rightly terrified. 'Awe is a word too little heard today. Too easily we mortals assume a position of hand-shaking familiarity with God.'[4] The seraph touches a live coal to the prophet's lips as a sign that his guilt has departed, his sin blotted out. This cleansing enables him to speak the word of God in what will be a challenging ministry. Later we are offered a beautiful picture of the prophet's sense of divinely empowered purpose: 'The Lord God has given me the tongue of a teacher, that I may know how to sustain the weary with a word' (Isaiah 50.4). Here we see divine compassion revealed through a human voice.

God's equipping is seen again in the divine response to Jeremiah's fear about his youth: 'Truly I do not know how to speak, for I am only a boy.' God's response brings assurance that youth is no barrier to the call to communicate in his name: 'Do not say, "I am only a boy"; for you shall go to all to whom I send you, and you shall speak whatever I command you. Do not be afraid of them, for I am with you to deliver you, says the Lord' (Jeremiah 1.6–8).

A similar theme is seen in the call of Ezekiel. He is tasked with communicating to a people who are opposed to God: 'the house of Israel will not listen to you, for they are not willing to listen to me' (Ezekiel 3.7). While this might seem disheartening, God gives Ezekiel the tenacity to speak with courage: 'I have made your face hard against their faces, and your forehead hard against their foreheads' (Ezekiel 3.8). Perhaps this is God's way of saying, 'Ezekiel, your ministry is going to be like bashing your head against a wall, but I will strengthen you.'

---

[4] Coggan, D., *On Preaching*. SPCK, London, 1978, p. 29.

Inspired by God, the prophets use memorable and colourful language, such as: locust imagery at the beginning of Joel; the tender picture of God teaching Ephraim to walk in Hosea 11; the boiling pot of judgement in Jeremiah 1; and the trampled vineyard of Isaiah 5. Preachers would be wise to ponder the richness of the prophetic word; God communicating in technicolour, not black and white. Here is theological justification for the model of preacher as artist; one who paints with vivid language, appealing to the hearer's imagination.

And on a really bad day the trembling preacher might take comfort that God can even speak through an ass (Numbers 22.28–30); there is always hope!

The Incarnation

'In the beginning was the Word' (John 1.1): the Word presented as a Person within the Godhead, the eternal originator of all things. This Word 'is unknown and incomprehensible apart from the historical figure of Jesus',[5] who pitched his tent among us (John 1.14). In the Incarnation God comes obliquely, revealing divinity in the vulnerability of a baby. To the fearful preacher the nature of the Incarnation is a momentous source of comfort; just as God accommodated himself to human form, unpretentious and ordinary; he breathes himself into everyday human words. 'Christ's continuing presence in preaching propels us towards an understanding of preaching that borders on the sacramental.'[6] The Word is present in the words of the sermon.

John the Baptist is 'sent from God' to 'testify to the light' (John 1.6–7). The Isenheim Altarpiece portrays this powerfully: John stands before the cross, holding an open Bible in his left hand. His right

---

[5] Barrett, C. K., *The Gospel According to St John: An Introduction with Commentary and Notes on the Greek Text.* 2nd edn, SPCK, London, 1978, p. 155.

[6] Quicke, *360 Degree Preaching*, p .57.

hand points to Christ crucified. John's index finger is exaggerated in length; the viewer is left in no doubt, John points away from himself towards Christ. This image acts as a symbolic reminder of the purpose of preaching: to point the listener to the fleshy self-communicating God.

'Our preaching, commissioned by the resurrection, is a continuation of the preaching of Jesus Christ.'[7] Jesus came into Galilee saying, 'The time is fulfilled, and the kingdom of God has come near; repent, and believe in the good news' (Mark 1.14). Here the Greek word for time, *kairos*, means an opportune moment, rather than 'time' in the chronological sense. There is urgency in Jesus' preaching. *Now* is the moment to acknowledge the rule of God in repentance and belief. Jesus is inculcating a new perspective orientated around God's kingdom; a realignment to dethrone all idols. Preaching that conforms to the pattern of Christ calls for urgency, challenge, comfort and subversion. In every sermon there is the potential for a *kairos* moment; *now* is the invitation to encounter God, *now* is the moment for transformation. This dynamic understanding illuminates the sermon as an occasion of divine encounter.

Using story, parable, question, pithy aphorism and powerful image, Jesus' words provoked, as well as comforted. His communication was never dull; preaching after the pattern of Christ means not being afraid to subvert expectation, nor to ask provocative questions.

Connecting with culture

Reflecting on a theology of preaching, it is worth pondering Paul's communicative strategy in Athens (Acts 17.16–34). Athens at that time was a small town living off its history as a metropolis for the intelligentsia, numbering Socrates, Plato and Aristotle among its

---

[7] Buttrick, D., *Homiletic*. SCM Press, London, 1987, p. 450.

intellectual heritage. Paul hits the tourist trail and notices, with deep distress, the number of idols dotted around the city (v. 16). What he does with this critique is instructive; he does not turn away to find a small like-minded clique, neither does he keep his mouth shut and his head down. He makes positive connections with the culture: engaging people, reasoning with the religious people in the synagogue and the folk he encountered in the marketplace. He debates with the Epicureans, who thought the gods were distant and disinterested, and the Stoics, who maintained that the supreme god is found in many expressions of divinity (vv. 17–18).

Paul piques people's interest such that he is required to address the Areopagus (v. 19); a council of the great and good; guardians of the religious, moral and educational life of the city. Boldly, Paul adopts an affirming and respectful tone in his address (v. 22b), using the inscription on the altar to an unknown God to build a bridge between Athenian religiosity and God. Note the apologetic thrust concerning Epicureanism and Stoicism: he speaks of God as creator rather than a disinterested deity or a series of gods resident in countless shrines. He points to the God who sustains life and is not dependent on human hands like some household godlet (vv. 24–25). Paul's argument turns to discussion of the divine call to repentance ahead of the day of judgement (v. 30). He speaks of the authority of the one appointed as judge being demonstrated in the resurrection from the dead (v. 31).

Paul's apologetic preaching connects content and context; he reads the cultural signs for a sense of the issues with which people are concerned, without softening his message. Some mock Paul and reject his words. However, others find their interest hooked, and some become believers (vv. 32–34). Similarly, the contemporary preacher needs to be alive to the ultimate concerns evident in popular culture, making bold connections between these and biblical revelation, without diluting the gospel.

Scriptures

How we regard the Bible will affect how we use it. If we see Scripture as a fixed, static deposit then we are likely only to mine it for teaching points, potentially allowing difficult verses to drop out of view. This approach can produce unreflective 'grab and apply' declamation: 'it says in Scripture and therefore . . .'. It is wise to be wary of oversimplified application that overlooks context and genre; Judges 4 sees a woman hammer a man through the head with a tent peg, but this is not to be taken as the biblical basis for conflict resolution!

The Scriptures are God-breathed conversation partners. They poke, prod and push us to listen deeply, wrestle, answer back and argue, seeking God's blessing in the struggle. The Bible often acts like coarse-grade sandpaper, tearing into our rough edges; there is nothing static here. 'Only when preachers interact with Scripture, engaging in its life with heads and hearts, can there be powerful preaching.'[8] We preach in dynamic interaction with the scriptural texts, allowing the Bible to challenge and reshape our agenda.

To selectively edit out portions of the canon because they are tricky is a mistake; nothing is off limits. We may find many biblical texts uncongenial, violent, frightening or baffling, but there are treasures to be found here, as we can see in the sermons in the pages ahead. Trusting in the empowering presence of God's Spirit through the preaching process, the preacher asks, 'What does this mean? What do we do with this? How does it speak to us?' Preachers need to summon the courage to go digging, confident in the God who whispers, 'I am with you always.'

The Scriptures have a normative and essential role in preaching: the written word shapes the spoken word; the spoken words help us to discern the presence of the Living Word speaking to individuals and shaping communities.

---

[8] Quicke, *360 Degree Preaching*, p. 52.

Human creativity

There is artistry in preaching that echoes the infinite creativity of God. This offers theological support for experimenting with language, sermon shape and performance. Being stuck in a sermon rut, unreflectively repeating the same homiletic method, can become tiresomely predictable and fail to appeal to listeners with a range of learning styles. Do we preach in particular ways because that's the way we have always done it? Creative preachers are willing to try new methods, and include people in preparation and delivery. If a sermon captivates the hearers' imagination, inviting them to ask 'What if?', and challenge the dominant narratives of the age, then the potential for deep spiritual transformation is present.

Performance is theologically important; how we deliver will affect what is heard. The creative preacher will ask:

- Will the sermon be delivered using a full script, bullet points, or note free?
- Where will the sermon be delivered from and why?
- Could the sermon involve movement within the space?
- How will gesture and body movement convey meaning?
- How might variation in volume, pace and pitch help the hearer to engage?
- Could the sermon incorporate music, visual image or symbol?
- How might the hearers be actively involved in the sermon?

Deep listening

The Shema is a central prayer in Judaism: 'Hear, O Israel: the LORD is our God, the LORD alone' (Deuteronomy 6.4). Jesus states, 'Let anyone with ears to hear listen!' (Mark 4.23). A similar charge is found in Revelation when the divine voice calls 'Let anyone who has an ear listen to what the Spirit is saying to the churches'

(Revelation 2.7). In each case the call demands focused listening; the application of deliberate attention. Deep listening rests on an awareness that the Holy Spirit is present in preaching, at the mouth of the speaker and in the heart and mind of the listener. Deep listening is an act of discernment: 'What is God's word to us, to me, in this present moment?' Failure to attend leads to a sermon stillborn in the heart and mind of the hearer. Listening matters.

> The response called for in the Bible to the hearing of the words of God is not mere assent, but faith in the God who speaks the promise, obedience to the God who commands, faithfulness to the God who has made his covenant plain, return to the God who warns, and hope in the God who foretells the future. To respond to God's words is to respond to *God*: God is present in the speaking of his words.[9]

Calling

Throughout the Scriptures and across the history of the Church we see God calling and equipping people to communicate his word. This calling does not airbrush out the character, personality and gifts of the preacher. God calls preachers to speak in their own particular accent, rather than adopt a false persona or a weird preaching voice. Conscious of having been called, preachers can have the courage to preach as themselves and the confidence to trust that they are never alone in this task; God enables.

Without sure theological foundations, the most 'secure' preacher is likely to wobble. Even with the trickiest texts, theological confidence means the preacher can trust that shape and content will emerge as the Spirit kneads the sermonic dough and knocks it into shape. Preachers can easily be affected by congregational response – either accolade or criticism, or the bland 'Nice sermon,

---

[9] Adam, *Speaking God's Words*, pp. 21–2.

Vicar'. It is easy to have a disproportionate sense of failure or success after giving a sermon. Theological grounding speaks wisdom into this. After all, 'Who gives speech to mortals?' (Exodus 4.11). Having a clear grasp of the theological foundations for preaching gives a sense of grounding and security when wrestling with tricky texts.

Questions to consider

- Describe your theology of preaching. Are there aspects of this chapter you want to challenge, question or develop?
- What is the story of your call to preach?
- Have you ever discussed with your congregation(s) the role of the hearer in the preaching event? What did you/would you want to say to them?
- In what ways do you discern interest in God in our culture?
- What is the trickiest text you have ever preached from and how did you handle it?

Part 2

SERMONS ON
TRICKY TEXTS

3

Beyond human experience

———•◦•———

God Transcendent,
beyond our human knowing,
grant us the faith to trust that
where our experience and vision
find their limit,
you are there and beyond.

'But these words seemed to them an idle tale, and they did
not believe them.'   (Luke 24.11)

How is the preacher to deal with texts that might be dismissed
as idle tales because they are beyond human experience? What
strategies might be employed to help a congregation willingly to
suspend disbelief and enter into the strange world of the biblical
narratives? How can the preacher help hearers to get past inner
objections so they can wrestle with the 'And so what?' questions?

The following sermons deal with other-worldly themes: a dead
man checks out of his tomb after a four-day stay (John 11.1–44);
Jesus goes all shiny and meets long-dead heroes of Jewish faith,
and the divine voice speaks from a bright cloud (Matthew 17.1–13);
people who were dead exit their graves and wander the city,
an angel appears and the crucified, dead and buried Jesus meets
his friends (Matthew 27.51—28.8). How do we deal with texts
that present us with events beyond human experience? Following
the sermons below we have picked out some homiletic strategies
to help in handling tricky texts.

John 11.1–44: The promise of life – eternal

JAMES DUNN

'Now a certain man was ill, Lazarus of Bethany, the village of Mary and her sister Martha.' (John 11.1)

The gospel of Jesus Christ holds out the promise of life. How better to illustrate that than a story of a man, Lazarus, who had been dead and was brought to life again by Jesus. And not just dead, but really dead. Other stories of Jesus raising the dead could have been based on a false conclusion. Jesus himself said of Jairus' daughter, 'The child is not dead but sleeping', when he took her by the hand and raised her up (Mark 5.39). And the widow's son at Nain had just died and was being carried out for burial – possibly a mistaken diagnosis (Luke 7.11–17)? But John seems to want to emphasize that Lazarus had really died. So, somewhat surprisingly, he has Jesus failing to respond to the desperate message from Martha and Mary, that their brother Lazarus was ill, for *two* days. And when he does go, as it would appear from John's narrative, to weep at Lazarus' grave (John 11.35), Lazarus has already been dead for *four* days. His body would already be decaying (11.39). So there could be no doubt. Lazarus *had* died. This was a real, an undoubtable raising from the dead.

John tells this story, at some length, to document one of the several 'I am' sayings he attributes to Jesus – for example, 'I am the bread of life' (6.35); 'I am the light of the world' (8.12); 'I am the true vine' (15.1). None of these sayings are used by the other Evangelists, and presumably were unknown to them – why would they have ignored them otherwise? They are sayings, then, that sum up the truth of the gospel and the way the good news of Jesus had no doubt transformed the lives of John and his community.

26

In this case Jesus says, 'I am the resurrection and the life. Those who believe in me, even though they die, will live, and everyone who lives and believes in me will never die' (11.25–26). How better to illustrate the truth of this saying than the story of how Jesus raised from the dead someone who had been dead for four days? Could there be a more powerful illustration that death is *not* the end? That the life Jesus embodies defies death? That those on whom he bestows this life 'will never die'?

Ah yes! There is a more powerful illustration. And not just that death can be reverted and put off to a later date. But an illustration of life that endures *through* and *beyond* death. And that illustration is the death *and resurrection* of Jesus himself. That is the climax to John's telling the story of Jesus – as it is the climax of the several tellings of the same story by the other New Testament Gospel-writers. To those who believe in the risen Jesus there is given a quality of life that not even death can end. This is certainly beyond our experience, but *not* beyond our faith and hope.

John brings the same point out by showing Jesus as regularly speaking about *eternal* life. It is of some interest that the other Gospel-writers remember Jesus as speaking of 'eternal life' on effectively only one occasion. That is when the rich young man asks Jesus what he must do to 'inherit eternal life' (Mark 10.17). It's a sad story. For he is a most admirable young man. When Jesus refers him to the commandments, he is able to affirm that he has observed them all from his youth (10.20). The one thing he lacks, says Jesus, is that he should sell all that he possesses and give to the poor. And the story ends sadly. For the young man was very rich and could not contemplate such a sacrifice. From which Jesus draws the more encouraging conclusion that his disciples have given up everything to follow him and will receive much more in this life, and in the age to come eternal life (10.30).

But that is almost all the other three Gospels say about 'eternal life'. They do not recall it as a regular feature of Jesus' teaching and preaching. In contrast, the message concerning and to the rich young man is one that John takes up. In speaking to Martha in John 11 Jesus does not use the phrase 'eternal life'. But in saying, 'Those who believe in me, even though they die, will live, and everyone who lives and believes in me will never die,' Jesus was certainly speaking of *eternal* life.

And it is this theme that John repeats and elaborates in his Gospel. 'For God so loved the world that he gave his only Son, so that everyone who believes in him may not perish but may have eternal life' (3.16). 'Whoever believes in the Son has eternal life' (3.36). Alternatively expressed, says Jesus, 'Anyone who hears my word and believes him who sent me has eternal life' (5.24). Note the present tense: 'has eternal life'. 'Eternal life' as something that begins, or can begin *now*. The clear implication, illustrated further in the raising of Lazarus, is that life given by God is a life that death cannot end, a life that endures – *eternal* life.

And what makes participation in that life possible? How does one come to participate in that life here and now? John's answer is clear. It is belief in Christ. That is, not simply a belief in a great religious leader. Nor is it simply an affirmation of the values and priorities of what Jesus stood for as admirable social ideals. But a belief that is the fundamental factor in life, shaping and determining the life of the believer. A belief in the Son that is a commitment to the Son, to live out his priorities and principles, with the inspiration and strength that only he can give.

John has Jesus putting the same point later: 'Do not work for the food that perishes, but for the food that endures for eternal life' (6.27). And he goes on to explain that there is a crucially more important 'work' to be considered. 'This is the work of God, that you believe in him whom he has sent' (6.29). This is what God wants: 'that all who see the Son and believe in him may have eternal life' (6.40). So, there is a 'food that endures for eternal life', and it has to be consumed. And it is consumed by believing in Jesus as God's emissary. Is John thinking here of the Last Supper? It would appear so. For Jesus goes on to say, 'Those who eat my flesh and drink my blood have eternal life' (6.54). But lest they miss the imagery and think of a too literal eating and drinking, John has Jesus adding a warning note: 'It is the spirit that gives life; the flesh is useless. The words that I have spoken to you are spirit and life' (6.63). It is the believing as an act, imaged by the act of eating and drinking, to which the promise of eternal life is given. Not simply saying the words of creed or liturgy, but absorbing them into one's very being and doing, so that the life lived expresses the life given, and the relationships shared.

John shows Jesus speaking about eternal life on other occasions. He likens himself to a shepherd and his disciples to his flock. 'My sheep hear my voice. I know them, and they follow me' – interesting to note that in those days sheep followed rather than being driven. And he adds, 'I give them eternal life, and they will never perish. No one will snatch them out of my hand' (10.27–28). '*Eternal* life' – that is certainly beyond our experience. And the raising of Lazarus is a stunning illustration of a life that does not end with death!

Or again, one of the most challenging things that Jesus says in John's Gospel: 'Those who love their life lose it, and those who hate their life in this world will keep it for eternal life' (12.25). What a challenging play on the theme of life. For those who think this life is all there is to life, and who see life as an opportunity to serve their own interests and to do down others – that makes life a negative sum game. Rather, says Jesus, those who do not see this life as all there is to life, those willing to spend their lives for others, like Jesus himself, they will find that this life is the beginning of eternal life.

And then John's final reference to 'eternal life', where Jesus in his last great prayer defines what he means by 'eternal life': 'This is eternal life, that they may know you, the only true God, and Jesus Christ whom you have sent' (17.3). This is what John means by 'eternal life'. For Christians, this is the heart of 'eternal life'. Knowing God, having a personal relationship with God, through

Jesus sent by God as his self-representative. It is the relationship that transforms this life into eternal life. A text beyond experience, yes. A life beyond our experience – well, that is the gospel's offer, for according to Jesus it is a life that can already be experienced *now*!

> Those who believe in me, even though they die, will live, and everyone who lives and believes in me will never die.

Matthew 17.1–13

MAGDALEN SMITH

'Six days later, Jesus took with him Peter and James and his brother John and led them up a high mountain, by themselves'. (Matthew 17.1)

Climbing a mountain is hard work. I know because I've done it. Over two days, stepping upwards into sweaty jungle heat I arrived at the summit of Mount Kinabalu – 13,438 feet – the highest peak in South East Asia. Climbing that mountain was exhilarating because it ended in seeing the sunrise. Our group, panting from a lack of oxygen, waited as the sun rose, showering our exhausted faces with a rose-tinted light. The same people as yesterday, we were subtly changed – charged with a brand new sense of achievement – our humanity expanded because of what we had done and seen on our way up the mountain.

People climb mountains for all sorts of reasons. Often it is to test, to stretch who we are – that deeply human yearning of going beyond what we think we can do – of testing our limits to the uttermost, whatever the cost. The film *Everest* tells the true story of two expeditions that attempted to climb to the summit of Everest in 1996. The film charts the danger involved in undertaking such a challenge, the responsibility that the two leaders, Rob Hall and Scott Fischer, had in retaining both the safety and spirits of those who chose to climb to the top of one of the world's most dangerous peaks. The film demonstrates vividly the immense perseverance the various characters display in attempting such a feat. Both Fischer and Hall die on the mountain due to a rapid decline in weather conditions, while others make it back down. One of the final scenes shows one of these men, Beck Weathers, being reunited with his wife Peach, the closing titles informing the audience that he lost both hands and his nose to severe frostbite.

Climbing mountains is dangerous because it has the potential to change us and change us big time. Perhaps this is why the story of the Transfiguration of Jesus in Matthew chapter 17 takes place on a mountain. The passage is notoriously difficult to understand, especially for contemporary readers. As Douglas Hare suggests, the story points mostly to 'a mystery beyond the reach of historical reconstruction or scientific verification'.[1] It is here at this high, 'thin' place where the boundary between earth and heaven is less distinctive that Jesus' physical appearance changes. Yet he does not become someone else, a god in human form, but God's power and light descend upon him, illuminating his humanity. Jesus is presented as the person who perfects God's plan, the one who will fulfil the vision of the implementation of God's kingdom. His life is 'shot through with God's, he is carried on the tide of God's eternal life, and borne towards us on that tide, bringing with him all the fullness of the creator'.[2]

Jesus chooses some of his closest followers to go with him up the mountain – Peter, James and John. Perhaps, like the Everest climbers, these men were ambitious for something new and momentous, enthusiastic to share something tremendous with Jesus, revelling in the fact that they had been specially chosen. Perhaps, after embarrassment over arguments about who was to be the greatest and after Peter's dimness and dissatisfaction, all of them were keen to show some new depth, and renewed guts. We have to give it to them in terms of effort. With the appearance of Moses and Elijah they are thrown into disarray. Elijah was the one who was meant to appear before the Messiah *returned* but here he is before Jesus has even left them! As so often, Jesus comes to the rescue in their confusion, explaining that God is allowed to redirect ancient prophecy and Scripture because things have not

---

[1] Hare, D. R. A., *Matthew: Interpretation – A Bible Commentary for Teaching and Preaching.* John Knox Press, Louisville, KY, 1993, p. 198.

[2] Williams, R., *The Dwelling of the Light: Praying with the Icons of Christ.* Canterbury Press, Norwich, 2003, pp. 6–7.

gone according to plan – the people are still sinful and have already disregarded the law (symbolized in Moses' presence) and dispensed with the prophets (Elijah).

But Peter is a practical man. He suggests building shelters – maybe because he wants to prolong this moment of numinous glory or because his tendency for denial is kicking in again – he really does see something strangely new in Jesus' changed form, and acknowledges that this is the beginning of the end. That although Jesus' shining face is a wondrous thing to behold, it also points to a darker pathway into an untold suffering. Maybe Peter just cannot bear this so he tries to extend the moment by building shelters, booths, places where this experience can be retained, held, cherished just for a little longer. It is such a human thing to want to hold on to those we love, even when they are changing. As our children flourish and blossom there is a part of us that wants to hold on to their energetic beauty. As our parents or our spouse changes because of terminal illness or dementia we desperately want to hold on to the people they are or were.

But Peter is silenced by the booming from the cloud – a statement that Jesus is God's beloved Son. For people in every generation here is a call to *listen* as well as to gaze upon Jesus in his glorified form. The Transfiguration invites us to experience a divine pause, an eternal unfolding in our midst – for it is an event that connects past, present and future together, a moment where God cuts through every boundary of time and space. There are times when we too may encounter something so momentous, something so filled with God that our sense of time vanishes. The Transfiguration is an event like this. The voice from the cloud reminds us of Jesus' baptism at the beginning of his ministry, and his shining face seems to catapult us to a future time of revelation glory and earthly consummation.

Rowan Williams, reflecting on the icon of the Transfiguration from the Novgorod School, comments on the significance of the event that reveals the depth of God's nature within Jesus' own humanity. Here God shows these imperfect and irritating disciples that God's life is compatible with *every part* of human life – past, present, future – from the terror of the cross to the glory of the resurrection. The Transfiguration tells us that the glory of God's holiness is to be experienced in our own humanity.

Looking into who Jesus really is can have serious spiritual consequences. We should expect to be transfixed by wonder, beauty and repentance; transformed, the experience potentially upsetting, overturning everything, who we are and how we live our lives. Williams comments that if we are not ready to be changed then we had better not look too long or too hard into the face of Christ. The Novgorod icon shows the disciples shielding their eyes from this event because they are simply not ready to look at the world in God's light any more than we are. This forms the basis of the theology behind Eastern iconography – the idea of adoring, gazing at the divine image – with ourselves passive yet openly receptive so that God can work within us. This is also the dynamic occurring here in this moment of holiness as Jesus himself remains strangely passive. It is the disciples who want to run around, fulfilling Scripture and religious history, having a purpose. But God, through the cloud, tells them to stop, look, listen before they plough on and stumble because they have not paid attention to a focal point of great importance – the divinity of Jesus manifested in human form.

We too need things that make us stop to see the depths of God in the stuff of our lives. Reading the recently published *Poems that Make Grown Men Cry* has ignited my own love of savouring words that are full of what it means to live in this holy and stained world. It has reminded me that we need to dwell on words that bring metaphor and emotion – that if we read too quickly we miss the depths, the profound beauty of the essence of each verse. We need experiences, encounters that make us stop dead in wonder, like the sun illuminating a stained-glass window. Wandering in the vast, holy spaces of our cathedrals and churches often causes us and others to pause – to catch our breath as eternity falls upon us like a gentle mist. We stop, sit, kneel and remain enfolded in an inescapable eternity. The Transfiguration was a chance too for the world to see through Jesus Christ into the depths of divine eternity in every moment of human experience and encounter. A divine and human person who stays in a place where he cannot be destroyed by emotion, culture, time or cruelty because his humanity shines, pulsating in the glory and mystery of who God continues to be and invites us to see.

Matthew 27.51—28.8

ROY SEARLE

'At that moment the curtain of the temple was torn in two, from top to bottom. The earth shook, and the rocks were split.' (Matthew 27.51)

It's more like a Stephen King novel or a Hitchcock or Polanski movie; darkness descending in daylight hours, the Temple curtain torn in two, earthquakes, screams, death, rocks splitting apart, tombs opening, the bodies of people raised from the dead, emerging from the cemetery and wandering around the city, a sealed tomb open, grieving women and guards fainting with fear. Weird or what?!

Just what Kermode and Mayo would make of it as a film is uncertain but it would certainly render an '18' from the British Board of Film Classification. But what genre is it? It has action, adventure, some comedy, yet more horror; it's an historic, epic drama set against a background of war. But is it fantasy or fiction? It's certainly an unlikely story, but it's true! It's not only the earth that shakes but it shakes the very foundation of our lives, transforms our existence and brings us to that realization that the gospel really is good news and that Jesus is truly the Saviour of the world.

The fact that it is such an unlikely thing to happen is exactly the point. Nobody dreamt or thought back then, nor should we think and believe now, that the resurrection was something that we can reasonably expect to have happened. No! It's crazy. It's an outrageous drama. It's beyond our human experience. It defies what we have come to expect. And that's the point of it. It is breathtakingly extraordinary, yet true.

It's a story that turns everything upside down and inside out. A drama that has the earth quaking and the world spinning.

A story that reminds us of God's victory, defeating sin and death, overcoming evil, revealing the all-conquering power of his love. A story that reminds us that God's ways are not our ways. He turns the values of the world upside down by his non-conformity to systems that dehumanize and blind people from seeing and discovering that fullness of life that he brings through Jesus to the world.

Among the first to recognize Jesus as being the true Son of God was the Roman centurion, hardly the religious type. It was to shepherds, marginalized, distanced from the worshipping community of those who gathered in synagogues and temples, that the angel appeared on a hillside outside of Bethlehem. And here we have another angel, a rock 'n' roll angel, a Rolling Stones angel, bringing good news, outside of the confines of religious circles. These big men, Roman guards, like the shepherds, were afraid. In fact they were so afraid they fainted so weren't around to hear the words that the angel spoke to the women: 'Don't be afraid.'

How extraordinary that God should subvert the protocol and ways of religious and civil society by revealing himself to women. Women, then not regarded as reliable witnesses in a court of law, are those to whom Jesus first appears. God is honouring women and commissioning them to be the first witnesses, sent by him to share the good news that Jesus is risen from the dead. They are central characters in this remarkable story and key players in sharing the good news.

We don't have to be reminded, as slaves used to remind their conquering masters, *memento mori*, 'remember thou art mortal', literally translated in Latin meaning, 'remember to die'. Death is inevitable and yet there is something about it that cuts across human consciousness. It comes as an uninvited guest, arriving on occasions when we least expect it, bringing an interruption and premature end to a story that was in the process of being told. It robs us of those vital components of human life, the capacity to hope, to have perspectives, horizons, desires, ambitions, ideas and intentions. To be alive is to possess the possibility of a future that reaches out beyond what seems inevitable, thus avoiding fatalism, cynicism, hopelessness and despair.

Christ faces death head-on and wins. His resurrection is the pivotal moment in human history. Without it our faith is useless and life is devoid of so much meaning. Sin has been defeated, death has been conquered, life has triumphed – that is good news! The birth, death and resurrection of Jesus are of mind-blowing significance. They mark hinge points in the history of the world. Matthew records the earth-shattering importance of Jesus' death and resurrection. Before Jesus rises from the grave there are three things in this amazing story that are like the trailer to a forthcoming blockbuster.

The Temple curtain is torn in two, from top to bottom. The curtain stood between the holy presence of God and sinful people. Its dimensions were 10 metres wide, 30 metres high and 10 centimetres thick. The fact that such a massive, heavy tapestry was ripped in two, from the top, about 25 metres above the floor, indicates that this was a sign from God. In the book of Hebrews the symbolism is explained. Jesus enters into the holy place through the curtain as the great high priest, sacrificing himself to pay for the sins of the world and thereby obtaining forgiveness for us (Hebrews 6.19–20). Hebrews goes on to explain that since Jesus has secured our salvation, there's no need of any more sacrifices and no need for a curtain to separate us from God (Hebrews 10.18–22).

The second sign was the earthquake. Its shaking was so great that many historians outside the Bible make reference to it in their writings, including Josephus and Pliny. When the verb for 'quake' is used in the Old Testament, it's used to describe the wrath of God coming in judgement. So we can imply from this that God is communicating to the world that while Jesus was on the cross, and judgement was being executed, the earth quakes.

And what of the third sign, these people who were raised from the dead and came out of the tombs and wandered around the city, recognized by many? That they 'appeared' doesn't mean they were ghostly mists or half-dead zombies. No, these were genuine living people. But what does such an experience mean? Why did Matthew put this in his Gospel? Well, first, the number of resurrections following Jesus' resurrection fits with Paul's teaching about the 'first fruits' (1 Corinthians 15.20–27). Jesus' resurrection is the ground upon which we can stand firmly in the assurance of our own resurrection. We can be confident and assured that we can know God's forgiveness and we really can be accepted into God's presence, that *we too shall rise with Christ*, that *even though we die, we shall live!*

So where does this amazing, beyond human experience story lead us? These incredible happenings, these awesome signs, symbols of the transforming power of God's love revealed in the death and resurrection of Jesus, should bring us to a place of worshipping the risen Christ.

The Roman centurion came to the realization that this Jesus was no ordinary man but the Son of God, the one who had removed the barrier between God and his creation, and the one who has made the way for salvation, conquering the power of sin and death. What the centurion meant by his confession, 'Truly this man is the Son of God', is uncertain, but we do know that the experience would change his life. He faced what all of us must face for ourselves: the question, 'Who is Jesus?' Do we believe that Jesus is the Son of God?

Powerful stories affect us in different ways. How has this drama moved us? Has it moved us to see that Jesus truly is the Son of God? If so, two things flow naturally from this.

First, the desire to worship, echoing the delighted cry – 'Christ is risen: he is risen indeed, hallelujah!' Second, the response of witness. The unsuspecting centurion discovers Jesus to be the saviour of the world and makes that known; the women at the empty tomb tell sceptical men that Jesus is risen. This resurrected Christ is at the heart of the gospel proclamation. This is the good news! As the song says, 'Go tell it on the mountain . . .', or to your family, your friends, your neighbours, your workmates, people near and far. 'Go tell it, that Jesus Christ is Lord!' Amen.

Homiletic strategies

1 Direct about otherness

James Dunn is boldly direct that his passage is 'other'. He points to the unequivocal fact – Lazarus is dead: decomposition has already begun. That's the point! The raising of this dead man illustrates theologically the Christ who leads us through and beyond our human experience and wildest hopes.

Roy Searle faces the problematic nature of the text head-on, calling it a 'crazy . . . outrageous drama'. Naming difficulty, speaking into doubt and uncertainty, causes a congregation to lean in, creating a powerful sense of the sermon as a journey of discovery. Searle shows similar boldness in naming the pivotal significance of the resurrection in human experience. Rather than being bound by what seems possible, he wrestles with the signs, seeking to articulate meaning drawn from close attention to textual detail; he allows the Scriptures to guide the sermon.

Even though both strange and familiar, Magdalen Smith acknowledges that her passage *is* difficult to understand. She succeeds in bringing the text within our grasp, showing how divinity is revealed in humanity; something of the life of God we too can embrace.

2 Scripture illuminating Scripture

Preachers will look in detail at the text in hand, but must remember that specific verses inhabit a broader text, and relate to a wider canon. Dunn locates his text within the sweep of John's Gospel, showing how the raising of Lazarus illustrates one of the 'I am' sayings, pointing to the resurrection of Jesus, and embodying the theme of life enduring through death. Dunn notably allows Scripture to illuminate Scripture, employing 19 references to texts beyond John 11.

41

3 Intellectually imaginative

The structure of Dunn's sermon illustrates a logical, clear, step-by-step exploration of the passage. Underlying the piece is an 'if-then ... this' pattern as he brings the strangeness of the text right into our living rooms. We can plot the stages in his argument:

- the gospel holds out the promise of life;
- Jesus declares 'I am the resurrection and the life';
- illustrated in the raising of a dead man;
- pointing to the climax of John's Gospel – Jesus' life enduring beyond death;
- Jesus often speaks of eternal life;
- eternal life begins through belief in the Son, expressed in commitment to him;
- such commitment is a life of service, knowing that this life is not all there is;
- the heart of eternal life is relationship with God through Christ;
- eternal life can be experienced now, and is within our grasp.

4 References popular culture

Such references signal that this preacher inhabits a recognizable world, even if aspects of the biblical world are beyond our experience. Smith uses the film *Everest* as a hook into her passage. Searle makes frequent reference to contemporary culture, mentioning Stephen King, Polanski, Hitchcock, Kermode, Mayo and film classification, bridging the gap between the ancient and the contemporary context.

5 Illustration

Smith begins with a personal, mountain-top experience, neither too long nor overpowering in the telling. Through her story she connects us to textual content with which we can identify. Her reference to an icon illustrates what the text itself demands: to be attentive and receptive to the divine. The use of a visual illustration, imagined or projected on to a screen, gives another way of approaching the text – particularly useful when a passage is beyond human experience.

4

Violent

———◆·◆·◆———

Vindicating God,
hear the cry of the innocents:
those abused, betrayed,
violated and murdered.
Open our ears to their cries,
our mouths in their defence,
our hands to their needs:
in the name of Christ
who trod the path of injustice
and overturned the powers of death.
Amen.

Heads smashed. A head hammered. A head removed. Hardly edifying passages! Ignoring them suggests there are aspects of human nastiness that can exist without censure, impervious to interpretation, beyond redemption. If we are to inhabit and uphold the gospel of grace we need to engage with these texts, as the preachers below demonstrate, wrestling Jacob-like in the darkness for the blessing of God.

Psalm 137

JOHN BELL

'By the rivers of Babylon – there we sat down and there we wept.' (Psalm 137.1)

'Happy shall they be who take your little ones and dash them against the rock!' (Psalm 137.9). Some years ago, a friend of mine was asked to preach in a prestigious, Edinburgh church of Presbyterian proclivities. It was a building sporting a large glass-encased notice-board on which the theme of the following Sunday's sermon was advertised in large letters. My friend, rather than suggest a snappy, seeker-friendly title, simply sent the text on which he intended to preach – Psalm 137 verse 9: 'Happy shall they be who take your little ones and dash them against the rock!'

He forwarded this to the resident minister, who informed him by return of post that while he was free to address these words in his sermon, it would be only the preacher's name that would be advertised on their noticeboard. Clearly in an era when terms such as child abuse and paedophilia had gained currency, it would not have been in the best interest of the church to appear to be beatifying those who would slaughter the innocents.

So, what do we do with Psalm 137? We could – as many do – simply sing the first verse as a mantra: 'By the rivers of Babylon – there we sat down and there we wept when we remembered Zion.' Boney M and many others have done as much. Or, if we regularly attend cathedral evensong, we may listen as the choir sings the complete psalm hoping, perhaps, to soften the offence of the final verse with the doxology: Glory be to the Father, and to the Son . . .

There is a third option. It requires us to do two things – to understand the psalm in its original context and to surrender our naive presumption that reading or praying the psalms should be a subjective, pleasurable endeavour.

Little needs to be said regarding the former requirement. Most people should be able to deduce from the text that this is a psalm of people who were forcibly evicted from their native land by the occupying forces. In 587 BC, the holy city of Jerusalem was destroyed and its people were taken in captivity to Babylon. It was there that they were taunted to sing a 'song of Zion', but they refused. It was not simply that they were unwilling to entertain those who had persecuted them. It was something much more profound. The German scholar Artur Weiser suggests in his commentary on the psalms: 'Not every place and hour, not every inward frame of mind, and not every human environment, is suitable for sounding forth God's praise. There are situations in which it would be wicked to praise God.'[1]

Whether it is in Babylon or in Guantanamo Bay, the praise of God will only be mocked if sung merely to satisfy the sadism of those who have no respect for the Almighty. It would be tantamount to blasphemy. It would be to suggest that faith and holiness were valueless.

Psalm 137 is not the praise song the captors wanted to hear. Instead it is a lament of people who have been so shot through with hurt and horror that they wonder whether God has abandoned them. So they, who have seen their children brutalized (for which we may read taunted, tortured, psychologically abused and/or raped), wish that a similar fate may befall the children of the torturers.

Not the words we want to pray

The sentiment of the request for the captors' children to be dashed against a rock, of course, offends us. We regard it as un-Christian.

---

[1] Weiser, A., *The Psalms*. SCM Press, London, 1962, p. 795.

We believe that such words are not befitting of those who believe that God is love and that reconciliation is the work of the gospel. This desire for revenge and retribution is alien to our religious vocabulary. If this is so, perhaps there is something wrong with our religious vocabulary. The celebrated ancient tradition of benediction or blessing is matched by an equally ancient tradition of malediction or cursing. It goes all the way back to the psalms, where there is no holding back when rampant injustice is visited on innocent people. For believers of the sixth century BC and for many believers all through the ages, private and public dialogue with God has to be grounded in honesty, not in evading the truth. Hence the psalms are forever calling on God to 'trip up by their own devices' those who create mayhem, spread malicious gossip or persecute the poor. For such people, not to be honest with God, not to declare a desire that the perpetrators of injustice be punished would be tantamount to endorsing their behaviour.

If I discover that a man in my street is beating his wife and abusing his children, do I simply pray that she will be given the strength to endure the blows and that the children will forgive their father? Or do I pray that through the intervention of friends, neighbours and ultimately the police, he will be held accountable and punished for the misery he has caused?

We should, however, note that neither in Psalm 137 nor in any other psalm that calls out for retribution does the author ask that God give them the opportunity to annihilate their opponents. Retribution, as Paul would later observe, is God's business. It is to God that the desire for vengeance is addressed in the hope that God, through whatever agency or influence, will rectify what is clearly wrong.

This psalm questions our prayer life; it invites us to be totally honest with God. It invites us to say what we want to happen if iniquity is to be redeemed through justice. And it invites us to trust God to find the appropriate means of retribution. This does not sound like the piety in which many of us were brought up. But it is the piety that Jesus was nourished by, and endorsed, when, as a devout Jew, he prayed the psalms, not just the pastoral and praise texts but all of them.

There is one other observation that might help us to relate to this psalm. It is simply that the psalms were not put together so that we might have words with which to worship our Maker. They were composed haphazardly for a variety of peculiar situations in which there were no words, no existing liturgy to represent an individual or a community on a particular occasion. There was nothing in the repertoire of the Jews prior to the sacking and destruction of Jerusalem in 587 BC to articulate the feelings of people who had been forcibly expatriated and demeaned.

The psalms record where people have been who have suffered from severe depression, from slander, from the predatory desires of powerful tyrants, from illness and from the fear of death. They are windows through which we are given a glimpse of experiences that, pray God, we may never have to endure. And as such, they are there to broaden our empathy and deepen our intercession for other people who are experiencing what the texts articulate.

I say this because of what happened one night in a study group when we were reflecting on Psalm 137. One girl, called Evelyn, was adamant that we should leave consideration of the text and particularly of the final verse as soon as possible. She dubbed it 'sadistic and sub-Christian'. However, the conversation went on a little longer with participants trying to discover what, if anything, was the value or the purpose of this text in our contemporary experience. All of a sudden, Evelyn re-joined the conversation. She said:

I've just been thinking. Alec and I have three girls. They are all under seven years of age, and it's very rarely that we ever leave them without one of us in the house. Perhaps once or twice a year on a birthday or our wedding anniversary, we might go out for a meal, and get someone to babysit for us.

If we were to do that, and returned to discover that the babysitter had not only abused our trust, but had abused our children, then maybe these words or something like them would be what I'd find myself saying.

And then she paused before continuing:

But I would never want to use these words unless something so unspeakably terrible had happened.

When we read or pray these words – 'Happy shall they be who take your little ones and dash them against the rock!' (Psalm 137.9) – we are given an insight into what those people feel like in Iraq, Syria, northern Nigeria and other places where women have seen their husbands and sons shot and their daughters brutalized. We are reminded of people throughout history who, because of their faith or their denomination, have become the victims of sadistic religious fundamentalism. We are offered the opportunity to understand what it must feel like to have all you hold sacred and those you most passionately love vilified and victimized out of sheer badness.

These words are not meant to make us feel good or bad. They are meant to deepen our prayers and activate the compassion with which God has gifted us.

Judges 4.4–22

KATE BRUCE

'At that time Deborah, a prophetess, wife of Lappidoth, was judging Israel.' (Judges 4.4)

(*The sermon begins at the lectern – at the opposite end of the space to the altar.*)

I need a hero. (I am not making a general confession.) Rather, in relation to the book of Judges, I'm looking out for that hero. A deliverer to break this downward drag of darkness and save the day. It has to be said, the day certainly needs saving: Chapter 4 begins with the old familiar pattern:

- The Israelites again do evil in the sight of the Lord. Things are going down, down, deeper and down.
- The Lord punishes them by putting them in thrall – this time to King Jabin of Canaan, and his commander Sisera. Talk about under your thumb for ever.
- The Israelites cry to God: 'Help!'
- Familiar with the Judges spiral, we have been set up to expect a deliverer to emerge. Hence I'm looking out for a hero.

Enter Deborah. Previous Judges have been introduced first by name and then by family relationship. To demonstrate, back in chapter 3, we met Othniel, son of Kenaz, Caleb's younger brother; and then Ehud, son of Gera, the Benjaminite (Mr Stabby), and Shamgar, son of Anath (Mr 'Come near me you Philistine and I will deck you with an ox-goad'). By the way – ox goad = pointy stick for prodding oxen. These are the macho, macho men of Judges.

(*Indicate a point to the right of the lectern, to position Deborah.*)

Deborah's introduction is a little different. First, she is named, then we are told she is a prophetess; finally we are given her family status,

50

as wife of Lappidoth. The writer also gives us a picture of her sitting under the palm of Deborah (her very own tree) between Ramah and Bethel, between the Northern and Southern Kingdoms. We are told, 'the Israelites come up to her for judgment'. There is trust here.

The previous judges are principally military men. However, Deborah is portrayed as exercising religious leadership, as a prophetess; political, moral and ethical leadership as a judge, *and* military leadership. She summons Barak and instructs him on military tactics. He even insists on her presence with him in the battle. Deborah understands that Barak fights for glory for himself, but she prophesies that the Lord will sell Sisera into the hand of a woman, a prophecy that seems fulfilled in the morally questionable actions of Jael.

Deborah – a remarkable, bold, courageous and commanding woman. And yet, Deborah's position in Judges is ambiguous. The text doesn't actually say that God raised up Deborah as a deliverer (a phrase used of Othniel and Ehud). Perhaps that was a step too far for our writer? *And yet* Deborah clearly seems to speak and act in God's name. The words she utters come to pass. Following the overthrow of King Jabin, we are told that the land had rest for 40 years, just like it did after Othniel's leadership.

The point is, whether the judge is male or female, sooner or later the people go back and do what is evil in the sight of the Lord. They do after Deborah's ministry, just as they do after that of Othniel, Ehud and Shamgar. The downward spiral of Judges is relentless. Don't get me wrong. I want us to celebrate Deborah as a strong, courageous and confident leader, but Deborah is not the deliverer I am looking for.

(*Indicate a point to the left of the lectern, to position Jael.*)

What of our tent-peg wielder, Jael? What to make of this sister who is most definitely doing it for herself? Jael is wife of Heber the Canaanite. It's important to note that there was peace between

Jael's people and King Jabin. That's why when Jabin's man Sisera flees from the battle on foot he seeks refuge in the tent of Jael. This should be a place of rest and refuge. Jael welcomes Sisera warmly. 'Turn aside, my lord, turn aside to me, have no fear.'

Sisera, Sisera. RUN AWAY. One way or another she's gonnagetcha, getcha, getcha, getcha. She's got you pegged, or she will do in a minute. In a gross betrayal of the laws of hospitality, she takes up her tent peg and mallet and goes a-hammering. This is one twisted sister. (*Look towards left.*) Jael, you're heading for Broadmoor. If we learn anything from Jael – I would suggest it is this: People, on bad days, when you want to sharpen your elbows and prove that you're the woman, you're the man . . . Step away from the tent peg.

I am still holding out for a hero/heroine, someone who will lift our vision to the source of deliverance that reshapes and trains the human heart for ever. This lies well beyond the twilight zone of the book of Judges.

(*Look up and gesture towards a place by the side of the altar.*)

As I stare out from Judges across the landscape of Scripture, a light falls on a particular place and person (*point ahead*). So let's go and visit her – and on the way we could greet a few inspiring sisters living in the landscape of Scripture. Deborah, Jael – you come too – but watch what you are doing with that tent peg. You'll have me eye out.

(*Move towards the spot highlighted. Use gesture to place the other women around the space on the way to that position.*)

There's Ruth . . . loved your commitment to the mother-in-law. Top courage. Great example.

Hannah, beautiful song of praise for God. What a theologian!

Huldah – great prophesying, sister.

Esther. Raised up 'for such a time as this'. Well played. Politically astute.

Lady Wisdom, you keep crying out in the marketplace. Wisdom *is* better than jewels.

Elizabeth, righteous, blameless and in God's good time a mother. Many congrats on the pregnancy.

Mary, Jesus' mum. Faithful, reflective, loyal and strong. Forgive us when we underplay your great significance.

Anna – with prophetic insight you recognized Jesus when others walked by.

Martha and Mary – great friends of the Lord. Honest. Real. Loving.

Elderly lady in the Temple. Modelling generosity – you put all you had in that collection plate.

Oh and over there Mary Magdalene – Apostle to the Apostles.

Hey Lydia – how's the purple cloth business?

Lois and Eunice – great parenting skills. You did a top job on Timothy.

Listen, let's all focus together on a woman (*gesture to an empty space by the altar*) who preached a knockout sermon without even opening her mouth. This unnamed woman is a risk-taker, passionate, generous and visionary. In her humility, gratitude and love she points us to the Deliverer of all deliverers, the hero we are all holding out for. Here she comes . . .

Hear the Gospel of our Lord Jesus Christ according to Mark 14.3–9.

While he was at Bethany in the house of Simon the leper, as he sat at the table, a woman came with an alabaster jar of very costly ointment of nard, and she broke open the jar and poured the ointment on his head. But some were there who said to one another in anger, 'Why was the ointment wasted in this way? For this ointment could have been sold for more than three hundred denarii, and the money given to the poor.' And they scolded her. But Jesus said, 'Let her alone; why do you trouble her? She has performed a good service for me. For you always have the poor with you, and you can show kindness to them whenever you wish; but you will not always have me. She has done what she could; she has anointed my body beforehand for its burial. Truly I tell you, wherever the good news is proclaimed in the whole world, what she has done will be told in remembrance of her.'

This is the gospel of the Lord.

Whoever we are, woman or man, teacher or student, ordained or lay, young or old, whatever – all of us are called here, to Jesus, where what matters isn't power, position or prestige. Here is the place to set down the tent pegs of (*as these sins are named, remove tent pegs hidden about person and place on altar*) self-righteousness, pride, selfishness, vindictiveness and self-reliance.

This unnamed woman points to what matters. She pours herself out in worship before the only Deliverer, the only one who can save us from the sin that distorts and drags us downward. Deborah is great – but she isn't going to save us.

Jael is strong – but her way is the cul-de-sac of violence and retribution. But this unnamed woman, in her anointing, worships him, Jesus Christ:

The one who poured himself out for us.
Friend of sinners.
Friend of fools.
Friend of tent-peg-wielding idiots.
Friend of women.
Friend of men.
Judge of the Judges.
Deliverer of deliverers.
Saviour of the universe.
Jesus Christ.

We don't need to hold out for a hero any more.
We already got one.
Thank God.

Mark 6.14–29: The birthday party from hell

WALTER MOBERLY

'Herodias had a grudge against John the baptizer, and wanted to kill him. But she could not ... But an opportunity came when Herod on his birthday gave a banquet.' (Mark 6.19, 21)

Violence. That is our theme today.

A major contemporary concern is the relationship between believers and others who do not share their outlook. It is frequently held that religious belief is likely to make believers *act violently towards* certain others. Whatever the merits of that charge (it only really gains traction from a few extreme cases that get wide publicity), our concern today is the opposite – that violence that believers themselves *may suffer from* certain others.

Such violence is part of the bigger issue of what we should expect from God. St Teresa of Avila is famously reputed to have said to God: 'Lord, if this is how You treat Your friends, it's not surprising that You have so few of them.' So what should we today be expecting?

Our story is a striking one, that tells of a strange sequence of events leading up to the death of John the Baptist. I would like us to linger a little on Mark's account and exercise our imagination, to get some sense of what is going on; and our imagination can be helped by drawing on further material from the Jewish historian of the period, Josephus.

To start with, something about our three main characters. First, John the Baptist. John we know about from elsewhere in the Gospels – someone who was preparing the way for Jesus by preaching repentance and giving people a fresh start through baptism (though as we are so familiar with the terms 'baptize' and 'Baptist' it might perhaps freshen our thinking a little to think of him as

'John the Dipper'). Second, Herod. The Herod of our story, ruler of Galilee and some territory further south across the Jordan, is one of the many sons of Herod the Great, and better known as Herod Antipas. Given the confusing number of Herods in the wider family, I hope it will help if I refer to him as Antipas. Third, Herodias. Herodias, clearly a woman not to be crossed, was another member of the large Herod family, and a (half-) niece to Antipas. She had only fairly recently married Antipas, having previously been married to one of Antipas' half-brothers.

Our characters are brought together because John denounced this marriage between Antipas and Herodias. Why did John oppose the marriage? In part it was no doubt because in biblical law there is a prohibition against marrying a brother's wife.[1] However, Josephus tells of how Antipas and Herodias had *both* already been married, but when they met and fell in love they *each* divorced their spouse so that they could marry one other. John may well also have been condemning what he considered to be essentially a manipulation of the law by the powerful so as to rationalize and legitimize what began as adultery (that may well also be the point of Jesus' words, also in Mark, about divorce and remarriage constituting adultery).[2] Anyway, for his pains John was imprisoned by Antipas at Herodias' instigation.

Then there is Antipas' actual birthday party. Interestingly, there are two rather different ways of envisaging what happens. The usual way, well represented historically in art and music, is to envisage the dancer as Salome, the daughter of Herodias by her first marriage, a young woman probably in her late teens. In the context of what was clearly a party of all male guests, it is easy to imagine a sexually charged scene: a curvaceous and sensuous Salome dances in such a way as to arouse Antipas and his friends; and their conversation becomes very largely of the 'Phwoar . . . !'

---

[1] Leviticus 18.16. Footnote references are for the reader's convenience, not for oral delivery.
[2] Mark 10.11–12.

variety. Salome might even have been put up to the dancing by her mum, who saw this as a possible opportunity to get something from Antipas. So it is a scene of a kind of sexual manipulation of Antipas to make an offer he then regrets.

There is, however, another possible scenario. There is a small textual variant in Mark's account in verse 22, when the daughter first comes in to dance. Some manuscripts have *autēs*, 'of her' (that makes the dancer Salome, the daughter of Herodias by her first marriage, as just outlined), while others have *autou*, 'of him'; this means that the daughter would be the child of Antipas himself through his marriage to Herodias, and that this girl is called Herodias like her mother. Since the marriage of Antipas and Herodias was still fairly recent, a daughter from this marriage would still be very young, either two or three years old. In this case, the dancing would be a tot running and prancing and waving, and delighting the adults with her childish vigour and innocence. Antipas' rash offer of up to half his kingdom (although a gesture with a precedent, since once King Ahasuerus spoke thus to Esther[3]) would be a fairly safe bet, as it probably shouldn't lead to much more than 'more sweeties' or 'Can I stay up late?' But the tot rushes off and says 'Mummy, mummy, what shall I ask for?' Mum, seeing her opportunity, says, 'the head of John the Baptizer', and her daughter probably doesn't understand this, but just thinks it sounds impressive and grown-up. An older teenage girl who knew about her father would realize that this would be a dodgy request for John's death and that her father wouldn't appreciate it. But in our narrative the girl 'rushes back' to Antipas in apparent excitement (literally, she goes 'immediately with enthusiasm'), and she elaborates her mum's words by asking for John the Baptist's head 'at once' and 'on a platter' – that she may imagine to be some special dish or delicacy just nicknamed after John the Baptist. She most likely has no idea what her words mean, or that her mother is manipulating her.

---

[3] Esther 5.3.

What should we imagine? A titillating teenage Salome, or a tumbling tot Herodias? There is a good case for both readings in verse 22, although the tot reading has better manuscript support. However, although I incline to the tot reading, the biblical story remains genuinely open to be read in either way. But whichever scenario we imagine, the outcome, tragically, is the same: Antipas feels trapped by his own words, and has John the Baptist beheaded directly.

The character of Antipas is also worth lingering over a little. For Mark paints a picture of a very recognizable type of person. Antipas is fundamentally a ruthless and self-seeking politician. He has no scruples about ditching his wife to marry a new love (even though his first wife was a political trophy wife with a powerful father who could, and subsequently did, cause Antipas real problems). He arrests and imprisons a popular preacher because he didn't like the fact that he himself had been rebuked, and because he wanted to please his new wife. Yet there is a part of him that is not corrupt, and that can recognize and respect integrity when he sees it. This leads to his actually wanting to bring a captive John into his presence from time to time so that he can hear him speak. However, John's position before Antipas seems well captured by the memorable words of the Lord to Ezekiel: 'To them [i.e. your people] you are like a singer of love songs, one who has a beautiful voice and plays well on an instrument; *they hear what you say, but they will not do it.*'[4] Antipas' recognition of John's integrity and holiness ultimately counts for nothing, as he cannot bring himself to act on what he (at least to some extent) recognizes as right. He has real power, power of life and death over others. Yet he is a weak and vacillating character, motivated at heart by self-serving actions and concern not to lose face. The trouble is: there are many such people in the world, not only then but now.

---

[4] Ezekiel 33.32.

Why is this story in Mark's Gospel? If we stop to think about it, it may be a little surprising to have such an extended narrative in which Jesus does not feature at all, and we hear about the dysfunctional dynamics of Antipas' and Herodias' family life. Yet there is surely a simple reason for its inclusion. The death of John anticipates and foreshadows the death of Jesus. Jesus' ministry, like John's, not only brings joy and hope and new life; it also engenders opposition, suspicion, hatred, and finally murderous violence. Nor does the Gospel limit such things to John and Jesus. Jesus spells this out explicitly and unmistakably: 'If any want to become my followers, let them deny themselves and take up their cross and follow me. For those who want to save their life will lose it, and those who lose their life for my sake, and for the sake of the gospel, will save it. For what will it profit them to gain the whole world and forfeit their life?'[5]

Let me put it this way. A phrase with wide resonance and recognition today, both beyond as well as within the churches, is to 'speak truth to power'. The trouble is: much of the time power does not like having truth spoken to it, and is apt to respond via its cronies and minions with varying levels and forms of lack of appreciation, many of which become in effect forms of violence – whether, say, the violence of verbal abuse, the violence of ostracism, the violence of neglect, the violence of bureaucratic silencing, the violence of financial ruination, the violence of imprisonment, or in some contexts even the violence of torture or execution. To be sure, powerful people can and do respond to words of truth; but such a response can only be hoped and prayed for rather than anticipated.

Put differently, faithfulness to God can be costly in our world, and the triumph of His good purposes lies through the valley of the shadow. A recurrent expectation, both outside and within the churches, is that if God is for real then He should sort out the

---

[5] Mark 8.34–36.

world and make it a better place, and also make better the lives of those who believe in Him. Yet somehow we forget, or fail to take seriously, the central image and symbol of Christian faith: the Roman instrument for the execution of dissidents and rebels – the cross. God's mode of sorting out the world is through the faithfulness of those who will embody His priorities in life and in death.

For most of us the forms that faithfulness takes will probably be mundane and undramatic: more persistence in obscurity than persecution in public or imprisonment. Most likely the factors that determine what happens to us will, humanly, often appear random – maybe even like a birthday party where dysfunctional family dynamics bring death to someone who wasn't even invited. We believe in the God of life. But we must live with trust and faithfulness to enter into that life.

Homiletic strategies

1 Use of humour

Kate Bruce deploys humour to acknowledge and offset the darkness of the passage, without diminishing its seriousness. Embedded are references to popular songs, employed to describe the narrative action and to raise a smile of recognition. Comedic conversational language, such as. 'Deck you with an ox-goad', 'one twisted sister' and 'watch what you are doing with that tent peg. You'll have me eye out', serves the theological focus of bringing the biblical narrative to life in the contemporary world.

2 Attention to delivery

The delivery of a sermon is a theologically freighted decision; the use of space communicates much. Bruce uses movement to communicate the idea of the sermon as a journey from violence to holy submission. The space between the lectern and the altar represents the landscape of Scripture. She begins at the lectern, making Jael and Deborah 'present' through the use of gesture, placing Deborah to her right and Jael to her left. Bruce then takes the characters on a journey towards the altar, pointing out women of God written into the biblical narrative. The journey leads to the woman who anointed Jesus' feet, with the Gospel reading being wrapped into the sermon. Jael, Deborah, the women of Scripture and the congregation are invited to gather in worship around Christ. The use of tent pegs as props, hidden about the preacher's person, allows for a moment of comic revelation as the preacher both expresses and invites others to surrender human follies, represented by the tent pegs.

With such use of movement, the preacher must be confident in the flow of the sermon and not overly dependent on notes. Using an A5 'menu' booklet is a helpful way of carrying notes as an unobtrusive aide memoir. This enhances the conversational aspect of the communication, facilitating ease of eye contact and a natural flow in delivery.

3 Respect for genre

Understanding genre and purpose is crucial to responsible interpretation. This is especially the case when handling explosive texts such as Psalm 137. John Bell addresses this concern directly, providing words of malediction, enabling the articulation of fury and lamentation in the face of the horrors of deportation. He helps the hearer by presenting contemporary situations in which the articulation of feelings of rage is both vital and understandable.

A crucial question to ask of any text concerns its purpose, both within the horizons of the biblical narrative and in the life of faith. Walter Moberly does this explicitly, asking why the account of John's beheading is in Mark's Gospel and revealing its narrative function of foreshadowing Jesus' death. He then uses Mark's reference to losing life for the sake of the Gospel (Mark 8.34–36) to explore the purpose of the story in the life of faith. The text demonstrates the cost of faithfulness on the road of discipleship, acting as both warning and encouragement.

4 Attentive to variant translations

Recognizing differing translations of the Bible opens up different interpretations. Moberly offers an unusual take on the more salacious interpretations of the dance scene in Mark 6 by drawing our attention to a small variation in the Greek text. In his convincing interpretation, a small child's innocence is starkly juxtaposed with her mother's murderous manipulative scheming, throwing into relief Herod's vacillating weakness. Competency in biblical languages is a real boon to the preacher, but a good commentary will highlight such variant readings for those of us less gifted!

5

Terrifying

God of compassion,
teach us to rage with you
on behalf of the powerless.
Hear our doubts and questions
as we struggle to comprehend
the darkness of the human heart.
Amen.

These next sermons deal with texts that should make us tremble; here we see power misused to devastating effect. How do we begin to deal with the rash vow of a triumphant general that leads to the burning to death of his daughter; a powerless woman given over to sexual abuse, death and dismemberment, to avert the threat of male rape; a father willing to sacrifice his own son at God's command; and a God who would demand such a thing? These texts provoke angry questions that need articulation and response. This demand is more than met in the following sermons.

Judges 11.28–40[1]

RICHARD BRIGGS

'But the king of the Ammonites did not heed the message that Jephthah sent him.' (Judges 11.28)

[A][2] Welcome to Lent.

Set the controls for the heart of darkness.

Meet Jephthah.

Our tale unfolds in three scenes. We'll take them in reverse order, given that the final one somewhat overbalances the narrative, and you almost certainly can't get it out of your head. So: fade up on scene three . . .

[B] We're with Jephthah, in the back of the stagecoach, returning hot foot from victory against the Ammonites. Slaughter against all the odds. Twenty towns laid waste. And a big hero's welcome, at the town hall, tomorrow, interview in the *Gileadite Gazette*, all good. Must go home and meet the family first, Mrs J, and his little girl, the apple of his eye, his one and only offspring, daughter of the all-conquering chief.

He's riding in the stagecoach, bouncing along, humming a happy tune, glancing to the horizon, slightly nervous, barely able to articulate the nagging thought at the back of his mind, that this has been one hell of a military campaign. He had felt the spirit of the Lord coursing through him, that exquisite sense that every exploit and every heartbeat had been dedicated to the Lord. Then, some-

---

[1] Core elements of the sermon were subsequently reappropriated for a written reflection, 'Frailty, Thy Name is Jephthah: The Tragedy of Judges 11', that appeared in Briggs, R. S., *Fairer Sex: Spiritual Readings of Four Old Testament Passages about Men and Women*. Grove Books, Cambridge, 2015, pp. 16–20, and we are grateful to Ian Paul at Grove Books for permission to reuse much of that text.

[2] The letters in the sermon text correlate to physical movement in the sermon delivery. See p. 83 for explanation.

Terrifying

where, perhaps when they'd just been rolling the landing craft on to the Normandy beaches, and his heart had been in his mouth, he'd flashed on thinking that he could show his devotion to the Lord by offering to dedicate to him the first living thing to come out and greet him from the doors of his house, when he returned victorious after the war, thinking that well, you never knew, maybe it would be the last promise he ever made, and maybe he would never make it back, and maybe God wasn't listening. But just in case, and just to do the best he could for his chances, he'd vowed a vow.

So there he is – bouncing down the dirt road to the imagined family version of the hero's welcome, but wondering who is coming out to meet him. Like Conrad's Marlow, sailing up the Congo into the heart of darkness. There's the sound of tambourines and singing, CNN is on in the background, the war is in the news, and there's a figure just emerging from behind the screen door. And the vow is weighing heavy on his heart . . .

[C] We turn back for a moment to scene two, earlier in the story. 'The spirit of the Lord came upon Jephthah.' The man of God – scratch that – the mighty man of God. A judge, a deliverer, a man who gets to play a part in the story of Holy Scripture, reserving his seat right there for the roll call of heroes in Hebrews 11. The spirit of the Lord. What a vote of confidence: mightily used in the kingdom of God. Think of the ministry possibilities, not least the chance to take his testimony on the road – 'Ladies and gentlemen, tonight, for one night only: "And then I felt the power of the Lord upon me . . . and verily did I slay the Ammonites, and hither and thither did we rock the Casbah".' So what's that about then? The enabling of the Spirit of the Lord unto death and destruction? Did we swallow that camel only to strain at the end of the story? Note to self: scene two a bit problematic. Let's try scene one.

[D] Here beginneth the lesson, reading from Judges 11 verse 1: 'Now Jephthah the Gileadite'. Let me attempt a rough and literal

65

translation of this opening verse: 'Now Jephthah the Gileadite was a warrior of strength; and he / was the son / of a woman / of immorality.' Yep: the son of a prostitute, fathered – as verse 1 goes on to tell us with typical deadpan truthfulness – fathered by Gilead, possibly using his tribal name to stand in for his actual name, perhaps he paid good money to remain anonymous, since his starring role is not a man's finest moment. Tough: in the process he also drags his entire tribe's name down with him. *Good old Gilead, Jephthah's Dad.* Gilead's wife also bore him sons. Except that Mrs Gilead's sons didn't much care for the son of the prostitute, and to cite the wondrous King James Version: 'And Gilead's wife bare him sons; and his wife's sons grew up, and they thrust out Jephthah, and said unto him, "Bugger off; for thou *art* the son of a strange woman."' Thus Jephthah finds himself in the land of Tob, meaning 'good', incidentally; kicked out into a good land (there may be a sermon in that, for another occasion), ending up surrounded by what the passage calls *anashimreyqim*, which the King James translated as 'vain men'; the NIV went for 'a group of adventurers'; the NRSV phones in from the Wild West to suggest 'Outlaws'; and the ESV, in breaking news from Cambridge, suggests 'worthless fellows'. Cads and bounders the lot of them. Those first three verses of chapter 11 are a brutal character portrait: son of a whore, kicked out by his half-brothers, spending his life in riotous living in some kind of supposedly promised land. Tell me, honestly, answer me this: is Jephthah a man who (a) grew up understanding the value of women and the need to treat them with respect, care, attention and love; or is he (b) not?

[A] The story turns around. When the war with the Ammonites comes, Jephthah negotiates his way back into the family, persuading the people to promise that if he wins the war, he can become their head and commander. Jephthah the judge. Has a nice ring to it. How great to be remembered for evermore by the people of God?

[B] So then. Here, at long last, Jephthah is coming home. Back from the so-called promised land, the outlaws and vain men, the squandered life, the hurting youth, the terrible back-story. Home he heads as victor, man of God, mighty warrior. Rattling along in the stagecoach, towards his own high noon, with the only cloud on the horizon, no bigger than a man's hand, the knowledge that he vowed that vow; but still, back from the dead, back from eating the food that was only fit for the pigs, back to triumph over the brothers who sold him into slavery, waiting only for the final triumph, the final affirmation, the final 'yes' to all his fears and insecurities, the figure of the welcoming father running down the road, the killing of the fatted calf, the embrace of eternity, the 'well done, good and faithful son' that he has so longed to hear . . .

The screen door slams. Her dress sways.

Like a vision she dances across the porch as the radio plays.

It's his daughter.

[C] Time freezes. The camera circles around them. No other sound is heard at this still centre of the oncoming storm.

'Alas, my daughter! You have brought me very low . . . For I vowed.'

And what's that she says in response? Is it something like: 'May it be to me according to your word'?

It's his daughter.

> *Kyrie eleison* – Lord have mercy –
> *Christe eleison* – Christ have mercy –
> *Kyrie eleison* – Lord have mercy.

Well, what did you come out into the desert to see? A sermon swayed by the wind? If not, what did you come out to see? A text of tall tales dressed in fine clothes? But what then did you come out to see? The truth? Yes, I put it to you, Holy Scripture compels us to face the truth.

[D] Now we all know plenty of visionary and inspiring passages in the Bible that lift our eyes and spirits to the far horizon, and speed us on our way to happier times. But we also know that there are passages like this, that point resolutely downwards, inwards, relentlessly, right into the heart of darkness.

We know we need this. In our finest moments, we know we need a God and a Scripture that has stared down the worst that we can throw at it, and that cannot be shocked by our terrors and traumas, by any sin we might manage to come up with – and yes, I know there are people in this world who believe that sin is just an old-fashioned idea and that we've all matured out of that now – but frankly, they've probably not chosen to be here this evening to welcome Lent by taking communion, and anyway it's not about your neighbour, it's about you, it's about us, it's about our own darkness.

And if there is a word of life here, it lies on the path that takes us right through the middle of all our failings, writ large, and touched and brought close to God by texts such as this.

[A] So all you mighty men, going great guns for the gospel, especially if the spirit of the Lord is upon you. Take care when you stretch to thinking that maybe your fighting the good fight will get you remembered in the history books. What will you be remembered for? It isn't about success. It's never about your own glory. And most specifically, it isn't about your mission mattering more than your daughter, your wife – your family – your household. Having a name in the history books puts you in the company of Jephthah. Is that really what you are signing up for?

[B] And, for all you wonderful women, there is hard news. The story of Jephthah's daughter could be speaking to and for you. If you haven't already experienced it, though surely you have, you will encounter the deadening truth that some men in power see you as part of their own power-play. Did you hear Jephthah's words when he finds that it is his daughter coming out to meet him: 'You have brought me very low; you have become the cause of great trouble to me.' That sounds so uncomfortably close to saying it's all her fault. Adam blamed Eve, and from that moment it has been ever thus. She accepts her fate, and bewails her virginity, almost certainly unto death, even though the hermeneutical lawyers are out in force seeking to commute the sentence to life in a nunnery. Personally, I do not think they will succeed. Would it have been kinder to hope that maybe all will work out for the best in the best of all possible worlds? Or is there release in knowing that, when it doesn't, you are not alone?

[C] But actually it's not really about men and women; or rather – the failings are not specifically or necessarily pride for men and prejudice for women. I've known women in power who have used words as badly as Jephthah did with his daughter, and I've known men ground into the earth by those who should have been their shepherds. So all in all, on this side of the resurrection, it's a tragedy.

Jephthah is a tragic figure. Locked into an inability to receive God's good gifts – the Holy Spirit; restoration to his family and his people – unable to receive them without adding to them a vow that will end up costing his family. In the heat of the moment: one tragic move, with endless consequences. Traced back, we have discovered, to his idiot father, father Gilead, who had many sons, one of whom was the fruit of his liaison with a prostitute. Another tragic moment, with endless consequences.

But is it not *good* news that Holy Scripture is there, ahead of you, when you finally find yourself in that darkest place?

[D] So to end: welcome to Lent. There are two important things you need to know about Lent. One: sometimes it is Lent. Two: other times it is not Lent. Time is not just 'one damn day after another', nor indeed 'one blessed day after another'. It comes and goes in seasons: of joy and despair, of fruitfulness and barrenness, of life and death.

[A/*now circling round and towards the communion table*] Today it *is* Lent. We offer ourselves in penitence, mindful of our sin. On the one hand, Lent says: 'Not so fast, hold the hallelujah's, there will be a time for them on Easter Day, on the far side of the journey we now undertake.' On the other hand, Lent says: [*now standing over the table*] 'Take, and eat; in this brokenness lies the light that is not overcome by the darkness, and the tragedy that turns out to be for the healing of the world.'

In the meantime, lament with the women of Israel, for the daughter of Jephthah is dead. It is not all right. Everything is not all right.

Welcome to Lent.

Set your course for the heart of darkness.

Meet Jephthah.

Judges 19.16–30

ALISON WILKINSON

'Then at evening there was an old man coming from his work in the field.' (Judges 19.16)

As a young Christian leader in my twenties I was asked to lead a Bible study held at the end of a midweek luncheon club at my church. After a hot, filling, homemade meal, and a substantial pudding, usually accompanied by custard, I expected my main challenge to be keeping the elderly members of the group awake. Uncovering great spiritual insights was not top of my agenda! I remember clearly the first session. About ten of us sat around in a small room in the church, and I glanced round at the group. Some of them were committed members of my church, whom I knew well. Others were from various local churches, whom I knew a little, and others were not from any church, just regular lunch club members who decided to come. I remember starting with a prayer and reading the passage, but I have no recollection what it was. Immediately one woman then said, 'Can I ask you a question?' I enthusiastically responded, delighted that I had created an open environment where people felt able not just to talk, but ask questions. She then went on to tell us the story of how, more than fifty years earlier, on her wedding day, her husband's best man had thrown himself under a train. Her question was simple. Could I explain why that had happened?

I still remember the stunned silence that followed, the shocked faces of those gathered, as our cosy afternoon was shattered by the tragic tale. These folk had come to talk about God, and have a pleasant time together. None of us had expected to face, head on, the desperation of a man who felt he had no option but to end his life so violently. We could only imagine the torment and anguish he had been feeling to act in that way. And even all these

71

years later, we saw the confusion and pain of a young bride whose wedding day, a day that should have been celebrated with joy, laughter and love, was overshadowed by the brutality of mental illness, desperation and a violent death.

A horrifying event had invaded the comfort of a church study group. More than that, its piercing reality had slapped us in the face. For some people the church isn't a place for such things. It doesn't fit with the stereotype of 'church'. Scones and tea. Smartly dressed people, with supercilious smiles, being nice to each other, in a bubble of polite British reserve.

But people of faith are not supposed to live in a fake two-dimensional reality. Instead, aren't we supposed to be people who see the world as it really is? As God sees it?

This passage from Judges 19 tells the story of an unnamed woman who is betrayed, raped and tortured, murdered and dismembered. This story is relentlessly bleak. She is treated as an object devoid of humanity. The nameless woman is pushed outside to a baying crowd of men intent on 'wickedness'. After being brutalized all night, she is dumped on the doorstep, before being dismembered and scattered. The brutality of the story is horrifying. There is no happy ending, and there is no resolution.

So why bring a story like this into church? Why allow these terrible things to even be uttered in the sanctuary? Why bring this horror to our attention? The command at the end of the story, the message that is to be sent out concerning this horrific description, is an indictment: 'Consider it, take counsel, and speak out' (v. 30).

We cannot pretend as people of faith that the world is a pleasant place for all. For many it is a relentlessly terrifying place. Most of us will at some point in our lives come across unspeakable horror, if not in our own lives, in the lives of friends, or through the medium of reported news. The temptation is to say, 'Those kind of things are unspeakable, so we won't speak about them.' However, this Scripture says, 'Speak about the unspeakable.' We must face this brutality. The Office for National Statistics reports that in the UK in 2015 two women a week were killed by a partner or former partner. Two deaths. Every week. Here in the UK.

Carolyn Custis James, in her book *When Life and Belief Collide*, berates the church in America for teaching fluffy theology, particularly to women.[1] I'm not sure the problem is just in the American church, or just with women being fed 'theology-lite'. This theology may seem attractive, but it has no substance and when life comes crashing in, it destroys the fluff and sweeps away faith in a God who doesn't engage with the horrific, brutal tragedies of this world.

Stories like the brutalization of this unnamed woman, contained in this Scripture, dispel any lingering thoughts that faith should be sanitized from the horror of this world. Rather, faith is lived knee-deep in the mess of this world, when we don't see a happy ending, with everything resolved.

We also need to speak about these terrible things because speaking about them brings them from the dark into the light. Only then can we face both the perpetrators of violence and brutality, and their victims.

The 2016 Oscar-nominated film *Spotlight* tells the true story of the *Boston Globe* uncovering the scandal of child abuse in the Catholic archdiocese in the Boston area. I came away disturbed with how well-meaning, 'good' people time and again failed to face the horror of what was happening, and ended up colluding, maintaining and facilitating the ongoing abuse of children. No one wanted to speak about the unspeakable. It's a tough watch.

Across the world, unnamed people have unspeakable horrors inflicted on them while we choose not to look. While we shield our eyes and turn our backs because it is too horrific, they continue to suffer.

As Christians we believe, preach and celebrate a suffering God, who in Jesus does not stand apart from the evil of this world. He

---

[1] James, C. C., *When Life and Belief Collide*. Zondervan, Grand Rapids, MI, 2002.

is not deaf to the cry of the oppressed. He is not blind to violence, rape and murder. He sees the exploited, the marginalized and our passivity and squeamishness with the horror of what human beings do to each other.

'Consider it, take counsel, and speak out' (v. 30) is the antithesis of passivity in the face of violence and brutality. It is a rallying cry, a marker in the sand not to allow the unnamed, unknown, faceless ones to be ignored, nor to allow their horrors to be shrugged off, tidied up or sanitized.

We left the story of my Bible study group in the shocked moments of silence, after the question, 'Can you explain to me why that happened?' I'm not sure exactly what I said, but it was a stuttering reply, saying something along the lines of, no I couldn't explain it. I was then interrupted by other people in the group, who first empathized with the woman, and then they started one by one to share their own stories of pain. They couldn't explain theirs any more than they could hers, but their gentle testimony of the long years they had lived was of a God who had walked with them in the horrors. The telling of those stories didn't answer that woman's question or remove her pain, but it connected her to others. It brought her pain into the open, and pointed her to a God who was able to engage with the horrible event, much better than I could.

So why tell the story of this unnamed woman in Judges 19? Why allow these terrible things even to be uttered in the sanctuary? Because such things happen, and people need to know they aren't unspeakable in the presence of God. Rather, to speak of these things is to recognize them, to name them as brutal, vicious and horrific. Speaking of them removes the shroud of silence on the victims, bringing humanity back to the dehumanized. It prevents us from slipping into a fairy-tale faith where all is well and nothing bad ever happens, all questions are answered and all problems resolved. Because they aren't, are they? '*So consider it, take counsel and speak out.*'

Genesis 22.1–19

GEOFFREY STEVENSON

'After these things God tested Abraham. He said to him, "Abraham!" And he said, "Here I am."' (Genesis 22.1)

No parent should have to bury a child. Think of the entrance of Shakespeare's Lear in Act V, carrying the body of his beloved Cordelia, made all the more poignant by foolish repudiation when she had failed to offer glib declarations of filial love. No parent should have to bury a child. Or Tolkien's King Théoden grieving over the death of his son. Or, in the recent film *Interstellar*, the hero travelling into the future by passing through a black hole. Although he is 125 years old, he looks 40 when he then meets his daughter, now old, on her deathbed. She sends him away, so he won't have to see her die.

No parent should have to bury a child. There is such profound grief in that loss: grief that time may dull, but never heal. Such a loss can split a marriage, with blame games or emotional retreat to where the other is not admitted. At every family gathering there is that sharp, gnawing awareness of the one who is absent and will never return. No parent should have to bury a child. And that tragic injustice is at the heart of the story of Abraham and Isaac, one that has engaged artists and resonated with believers down the ages.

A tricky text

Yet for moderns this is a difficult text. As soon as one takes even a tiny step away from the context, the story of a man commanded by God to take a son on a three-day journey to sacrifice him is almost impossible to hear. So many questions erupt. What father would even consider killing the son 'whom he loved'? What God would require that of a father and faithful servant, one to whom that very child had been promised to found a people? What child would willingly submit to being bound and readied for slaughter? And why is it only male characters involved? The listener has every right to ask such questions, but must do so within the great sweep of the biblical narrative and its teaching, and by attempting to understand the historical context and the early cultures of the biblical texts.

Progressive revelation

'Cosmic child abuse' is a phrase that has reverberated through contemporary theological debates, and with reason. This story, with other biblical stories of the offering of the firstborn, has been used, implicitly or explicitly, to support practices now unacceptable. One modern response is to say that the God of this text is not the God of the Christian faith. Or that at best, while the understanding and representation of the revelation of God was profound and perhaps even progressive for the founding stories of the people of Israel, that revelation has been refined and, in important ways, superseded by the revelations given to the Prophets, found in the teaching and example of Jesus, and in the writings of Paul and the Church Fathers.

Child sacrifice as a means of worshipping other deities is condemned and forbidden elsewhere in the Old Testament. Some modern commentators point out that from a context where child sacrifice seems to have been common, especially in Canaan, it is significant that in the end it was not a child but a ram that was sacrificed.

So one wonders, is God often one step ahead of culture (and two steps ahead of the Church)? Through Yahwism (the monotheism of the early Israelites), God was ahead of the surrounding religious cultures. God seems to have been ahead of Abraham on his journey – perhaps God was ahead of him ethically as well. It would be hundreds, if not thousands, of years before animal sacrifices were no longer required in Judaism. Perhaps God was ahead of Judaism when the scapegoating requirements of Torah were superseded for Christians by the one sacrifice for all. Sometimes, shamefully, God has been ahead of the Church, as in the condemnation of slavery, and in the move to equality not limited by race or gender. We might ask: 'Is God ahead of the Church of today, in our understanding of what is essential to the right practice of religion and relationships, and what should and should not be a matter of division?'

Then there is 'The Test', and God's need to prove Abraham's faith. It makes God sound quite tricksy and only too human. Can God in fact be trusted to fulfil his promises that depended on Isaac, and might come to nothing if Isaac was killed? Abraham has to trust God for this, as well as for his own love, gratitude and possibly grief as a parent.

But we must not read this story through spectacles that frame God as simply an all-powerful, all-knowing tyrant who must be obeyed. Nor is God playing a game with Abraham: 'Aw come on Abraham, thou shouldst lighten thou up. I was only testing thee. And thou should have seen thy face!'

A relationship marked by love more than power

Through the whole scriptural witness, God's relationship with his creation and his people is fundamentally marked by love, rather than power, and love is not without risk. God genuinely does not know the outcome. His words to Abraham, 'Now that I know', suggest that the testing, however repellent to our ears, uncovers something that could not be known in any other way. God had chosen Isaac to be the means of fulfilling his promise to Abraham. Israel is God's own beloved 'firstborn', and it seems – if we may be permitted to understand God in human analogies – that God is taking a huge risk. Abraham has been faithful and courageous, in leaving his land and setting out trusting a promise, but he has also been weak and duplicitous, passing his wife off to Pharaoh as a sister. God is taking a risk, and such a God is closer to the

God whom Jesus teaches and knows, trusting in God's father heart, and who taught, 'If you then, who are evil, know how to give good gifts to your children, how much more will the heavenly Father give the Holy Spirit to those who ask him!' (Luke 11.13).

It is Abraham as a father preparing to lose his son that we can't help wondering about. I would like to speculate on Abraham's thoughts as he trudges on. These are snapshots, unconnected, possibly not even from the same Abraham. There is precedent, from Origen to Kierkegaard, although with such a masterful literary text as Genesis 22, the preacher risks being like an artist blu-tacking his painting to the gilt frame of a Rembrandt.

> Why on earth did I not ask Sarah? She would have kept us from this journey. Now, when we are on our way, why do I not tell Isaac? All the way as we have walked into the hills, I have kept it from him.
>
> He must never know what I am going to do. He must never know an angel told me to do this. Then he might die cursing God. I could not let that happen.
>
> Far better he curses me. Far, far better he thinks his father has gone mad, has gone back to the old days of bloodlust and child sacrifice.
>
> So that is what I will tell him. As we climb the hill, just the two of us. As he hands me the wood for the fire. When I bind his hands, when I raise the knife. He must not know this is God. He would not understand.
>
> God, I will keep Isaac from cursing you. That much I will do for him.

Or else:

> The boy looks at me with fear in his eyes. He questions. 'If this is to be a sacrifice, where is the animal?'
>
> 'Jehovah Jireh,' I said, 'God provides. Has done. Will do. We will see.'

Isaac is quiet. He does not argue. He believes me. He trusts me.

Tomorrow we will be in the hills. God will show me the one we should climb. He will ask me to use the fire I have brought. And the knife. Tomorrow God will give the courage to do what I surely could not do today. Tomorrow God will provide. Jireh.

We will see.

A third interior monologue:

How could it *possibly* have been God who ordered me to do this? God who loves . . . God who blesses . . . God who promises . . . God who protects, nurtures, grows, encourages.

How could this test come from the God who made his covenant with me: lands upon lands. Innumerable descendants? This journey will end it all. I do not understand. I am afraid. I doubt. How I doubt . . .

And yet . . . isn't God more true and more certain than my doubt? If I somehow have it badly wrong – can I not trust God to put it right, before it is too late? Somehow? As we climb the hill . . . Somehow? As we lay the fire. Somehow?

As I raise the knife? Somehow?

Yes. How could my doubt defeat God? He would not let that happen.

Finish

Did Abraham wrestle in this way with his doubt and his fear? We have no way of knowing. But to me such doubt feels more true, more honest, and worth more to God than blind certainty. His will be a tested, tempered faith, forged in fire.

There is also much in this story about fatherhood and about loss, emotions almost too deep for words. The obedience and trust of Abraham, indeed that of son Isaac, resonates with the obedience of Jesus, on his way to the cross, and all is folded into relational love.

This obedience unto death prefigures and gives meaning to the sacrifice of every one of the Church's martyrs, even and perhaps especially those happening today. Such trusting obedience calls to us, not as a grisly and impossible command or tricksy test, but as an invitation to trust and to love a God who is intimate and approachable as well as unimaginably vast. Love cannot be commanded, but it can be drawn. Trust cannot be put into words – not convincingly – but only shown in actions. May our words and our actions draw us closer to the God of love.

Homiletic strategies

1 Pastoral empathy

Richard Briggs' sermon demonstrates the importance of careful scripting of a sermon, particularly when the challenges of the text might tread on the holy ground of people's own suffering. Casual phrasing or throwaway attempts at elaboration can cause inadvertent damage. The same is true of Geoffrey Stevenson's sermon. He acknowledges the awfulness of the passage, while wrestling to uncover redemptive themes and signposts. The layered repetition in the sermon's opening move, 'No parent should have to bury a child', empathically underscores the potential pain and outrage of the text.

2 Personal illustration

David Buttrick declares that 'there are virtually no good reasons to talk about ourselves from the pulpit', seeing it as a form of 'intrusion on our own sermons'.[1] However, Alison Wilkinson demonstrates that personal illustration, used wisely, can be extremely effective. Her opening anecdote offers us a peaceful, everyday scene – a women's Bible study – suddenly shattered by an 'anecdote within the anecdote', intruding on the scene with a story of unimaginable pain, suffering and grief. Wilkinson uses this to illustrate the situation in the text itself, where a man comes home from working in the field, the end of a predictable day, until a different narrative cuts across the picture with the horrific violation and murder of a powerless woman. Wilkinson chose not to airbrush out the painful question from the woman in the Bible study. Equally, the Bible will not edit out the nastier aspects of human behaviour: personal story can powerfully illustrate.

---

[1] Buttrick, D., *Homiletic*. SCM Press, London, 1987, pp. 142–3.

3 Writing for the ear

Briggs writes such that the listener is enabled to see through their ears. He orchestrates image and pace, with the eye of a film director. Underlying the whole piece is the extended metaphor of a movie, with flashback and fast forward, the camera zooming in and panning out.

The opening section is written to be delivered at high speed, to communicate restless unsettledness. The sermonic tempo creates and sustains tension; image upon image flash by in a blur as we travel home on the stagecoach with Jephthah. At the line 'It's his daughter', the pace abruptly stops at the freeze-framed horror of unfolding truth.

Anachronistic images elide the horizons of text and context: the Normandy landings, CNN and, for those with ears to hear, there is Bruce Springsteen, Forrest Gump, the Clash, Jane Austen, *Hamlet*, and more. Like these references, allusions suggesting other biblical narratives, notably Joseph and his brothers, and the prodigal son, add other notes into the score of the sermon; all can hear the melody line and some may delight in the witty harmonies.

Wilkinson's sermon is a carefully crafted lyrical piece; the imagery is powerful and the text has a rhythmic quality. She paints with words: 'faith is lived knee-deep in the mess of this world' and 'shroud of silence on the victims', more than exemplify this. The lyrical layering of images in the following example shows the power of language to puncture pretension: 'Smartly dressed people, with supercilious smiles, being nice to each other, in a bubble of polite British reserve.' Wilkinson capitalizes on the rhythmic nature of language, sometimes adopting a staccato pace to underline a stark point: 'Two deaths. Every week. Here in the UK.'

4 Internal monologues

Stevenson's imaginative use of three internal monologues opens up interpretive possibilities as we are invited to empathize with

Abraham's situation. These snapshots present Abraham as a loving father and a man of faith, wrestling, as we do, with the seeming contradiction in the divine test.

5 Using movement to narrate action

Preaching in the round, with a circular communion table at the centre, Richard Briggs used movement to help narrate action. Imagine the four points of the compass as A, B, C and D, each one situated inside the circle of the congregation, facing the communion table, and at the head of each 'aisle' between the seating. The points at which Briggs moved to these four locations are marked in the sermon above. The result was that the various episodes and perspectives of the text were all recounted from different spaces; re-circling the table allowed a sense of reprising perspectives made earlier. In the final section, the preacher approached the table, and finished with hands held wide open over the elements. The eucharistic setting enabled the sermon to be preached as Christian good news, allowing the text's focus on tragedy to be taken up into a wider act of memorial and celebration.

6

Strange

———◆•◆•◆———

Spirit of God,
brood over us;
as we step into
the strange world of the Bible,
bring to birth new vision.
Illuminate our insight
and grant us wisdom
to interpret your Word.
Amen.

A sumptuous party is interrupted by the weird sight of the fingers of a human hand writing strange words on a wall. A priest has a bejewelled breastplate made, studded with 12 precious stones. The wind of God sweeps over the waters of chaos. Supernatural strangeness, alien liturgical practices, and insight into what, humanly speaking, could not be witnessed: the act of divine creation 'in the beginning'; the passages in this chapter seem far away from our workaday world. However, the following sermons successfully allow the concerns of these strange texts to speak into the contemporary context.

Daniel 5: The writing on the wall[1]

JOLYON MITCHELL

'King Belshazzar made a great festival for a thousand of his lords, and he was drinking wine in the presence of the thousand.' (Daniel 5.1)

Take a look. It's Rembrandt's great painting *Belshazzar's Feast*.[2] It's sometimes called *The Writing on the Wall*. What do you see? There's gold, there's silver, expensive clothes, a remnant of a feast on the table. The wealth is hard to miss: painted in 1635, during the era of the so called Dutch Golden Age. Yes, there was darkness, the plague still struck, wars rumbled on in the first half of the century; but here we glimpse the comfort and prosperity of the

[1] Adapted from a sermon preached at St James the Less, Leith, Edinburgh, November 2015.
[2] Rembrandt's painting *Belshazzar's Feast* hangs in the National Gallery in London. Reproduced by permission. Copyright © FineArt / Alamy Stock Photo.

seventeenth century, with its embarrassment of riches,[3] a time that can still speak to many parts of our world today.

In this painting we're brought close. It's like a close-up news photo. It's intimate. There's shock, fear on faces, surprise in their postures. Gazes directed upwards towards bright semi-golden writing. Look closely at where Belshazzar's hand rests: on a golden up-turned platter. It's stolen gold from the Temple. He is clutching, but cannot grasp it. Notice how he knocks over a goblet. Liquid drains downwards.

Or there, look at the woman in the red dress. She holds a solid precious goblet. But it cannot retain its liquid, it pours out like a waterfall. In his book, *Rembrandt's Eyes*, Simon Schama describes this as like the 'liquidation of power'.[4] The king's rule, his power, is poured out. Symbols of stolen power are emptied. Rembrandt shows us how *all* rulers' power will eventually come to an end . . .

Listen again to the book of Daniel, bringing us close into the story: 'They drank the wine and praised the gods of gold and silver, bronze, iron, wood, and stone.' (Daniel 5.4)

Let's stay with *gold* for a moment. Can you remember where else gold comes in Daniel? Yes, Nebuchadnezzar's troubling dream of a golden-headed statue (Daniel 2). In the following chapter, Nebuchadnezzar has a huge golden statue built (Daniel 3). Remember how risk-takers Shadrach, Meshach and Abednego are made to bow down to this gold statue. They won't do it, so they're thrown into a fiery furnace, and . . . they survive. Protected by God they do not melt. Back to Daniel 5. Notice how gold continues to pop up. For example, Daniel is offered a gold chain around his neck if he can interpret the dream. Gold is portrayed here as worth working for, an incentive, the ultimate reward.

---

[3] See, for example, Schama, S., *The Embarrassment of Riches: An Interpretation of Dutch Culture in the Golden Age.* HarperPerennial, London, 2004.

[4] Schama, S., *Rembrandt's Eyes.* Penguin, London, 1999, p. 418.

In Rembrandt's painting you can see that Belshazzar has a huge gold chain around his neck; but in Daniel we read: 'The king's face turned pale, and his thoughts terrified him. His limbs gave way, and his knees knocked together' (Daniel 5.6). There's an interesting contrast between the apparent solidity of the gold and the paleness and the distortion of his face. Though it's a bit late for him to learn that 'all that glitters is not gold'.

In passing, it's worth thinking about how natural it is to put *trust in stuff*. Because we can see it, we can touch it; we can feel secure under it, or with it. No wonder the dream of winning a golden lottery ticket appeals. Why? Because we would be able to change everything, to escape, to be free, to do good, while building security for ourselves, those we love and those in need. And yet this story puts a question mark over this kind of dreaming and trust. It offers an alternative, critical vision. Notice how Daniel says to the assembled company, 'You have praised the gods of silver and gold . . . but the God in whose power is your very breath, and to whom belong all your ways, you have not honoured' (Daniel 5.23). Belshazzar had put his trust in inherited, stolen gold. He seeks to hold on to his own power, his worldly success, but hasn't humbled himself, hasn't put his hands out towards the living God.

It may not be gold, it may instead be our credit cards or the stuff we have, that we cling on to in our hands and imaginations. It's a risk to let go of 'gold' and yet the claim here is that it's *God* who holds us and history in his hands.

What else strikes you about the picture?

Perhaps you notice Belshazzar's very big hat. It's more than a crown, isn't it? It's a bejewelled turban with a crown on the top. Rubies. Crystals. Gems. But the crown is beginning to tumble off. A king in trouble. How the mighty tumble.

So the wine is falling, the crown is falling. By contrast the rest of the picture has an ascending motion, a movement up towards the bright golden top right-hand corner. And yes, following the gaze of the characters, our gaze is obviously directed upwards, towards the writing on the wall. Now look closely at the illuminated text, which reads, 'MENE, MENE, TEKEL, and PARSIN' (Daniel 5.25). It's complicated because these words are in Aramaic – the language of Babylon. Written not across but downwards. You may remember what these coded words mean? It makes no sense at all to the local wise men. And Daniel is offered incentives, rewards, if he can interpret them: purple, gold chain and third place in the kingdom. The risk-taker Daniel's reply: 'No, keep them for yourself or give them to someone else.' But he still reverses Babel's curse, and translates,[5] interprets . . .

They are actually the names of measures; they are monetary weights, these are nouns that he turns into verbs: numbered, numbered, weighed, divided. Here is what these words mean: 'MENE, God has numbered the days of your kingdom and brought it to an end; TEKEL, you have been weighed on the scales and found wanting. PERES, your kingdom is divided and given to the Medes and Persians' (Daniel 5.26–28). This is not good news. This is curtains. And the prediction comes to pass.

There's something about this story that's inspired artists like Rembrandt, but has also inspired musicians like Johnny Cash, who crooned 'Weighed in the balance and found wanting' (1964). You'll perhaps also remember how Simon and Garfunkel famously sang about prophetic words written on the walls of subways in their 1964 song, 'The sound of silence'.[6]

---

[5] See Hilton, M., 'Babel Reversed – Daniel Chapter 5', *Journal for the Study of the Old Testament* 66 (1995), pp. 99–112. For Rabbi Hilton 'the story of "The Writing on the Wall" is central to the book of Daniel, and dates from Maccabean times. The historical setting is precise, the night of the fall of Babylon in 539 BCE. Genesis 11 describes the founding of Babel (Babylon) and Daniel 5 the destruction of the same city. Both stories depend on a confusion of languages, but only Daniel has the insight to interpret it' (p. 112).

[6] At this point, the congregation unexpectedly started singing the song in harmonies.

So why has this story intrigued so many?

One reason is that it raises profound questions about how God communicates. Does God communicate through bright writing on the wall? Well in my experience, not regularly. Does God communicate through interruptions, through 'the still small voice', through 'the sound of silence', through paintings, through words and *the* Word?

Last night I saw the Riding Lights' play *Baked Alaska*. A line stayed with me: 'Climate Change is the writing on the wall.'[7] For Naomi Klein, climate change 'changes everything'. Perhaps the writing is on the wall for us who call this fragile small blue planet 'home'. Perhaps the writing is inscribed in recent floods, storms and distant droughts, even more than we realize or want to face.

Who else drew on walls? Well, the persecuted early Christians did. Let me invite you to their underground catacombs near the city of Rome. Daniel often appears on the walls, particularly Daniel in the lion's den and the trio in the fiery furnace. Why do you think the early Christians would represent them? Why would they draw on the wall about Daniel?

They had a strong belief in the resurrection. And these Daniel stories were seen as anticipations of the resurrection – people who should have died but who 'came back to life', out of the tomb, or out of the den of lions. The writing was on the wall for them, but it was reversed. Above these subterranean pictures you can sometimes see true gold, the Greek letters on some ceilings: alpha and omega, the beginning and the end. So here the early Christians are putting on the wall affirmations about God's place in relation to time and history. The writing on the wall extends our vision

---

[7] This assertion is made by the 'Prophet' character in the context of reflections on the future of the fossil fuel industry at the end of the First Act of Bidgood and Burbridge's play *Baked Alaska*, performed by the Riding Lights Theatre Company in Edinburgh on 20 November 2015. Reproduced by permission.

beyond last week's gold, or next week's goals, to a much longer view of history.

More recently there have been over twenty pop songs with the title of 'The writing's on the wall'. The phrase has become part of common idiom. It's there in the title song for the latest James Bond film, *Spectre* (2015). In it Sam Smith sings about taking risks for another because 'the writing's on the wall.' There are some people who take extraordinary risks to love and serve other people.

Mother Teresa, risk-taker and nun, is now not without her critics, but written on the wall of her cramped room in Calcutta is arguably true gold. Probably adapted from another prayer, this is what she inscribed. Let's read it together:

> People are often unreasonable, irrational and self-
>   centred
> Forgive them anyway.
> If you are kind, people may accuse you of selfish
>   ulterior motives,
> Be kind to them anyway.
> If you are successful you will win some faithful
>   friends and some genuine enemies,
> Succeed anyway.
> If you are honest and sincere, people may deceive you,
> Be honest and sincere anyway.
> What you spend years creating, others could destroy
>   overnight.
> Create it anyway.
> If you find serenity and happiness, some may be
>   jealous,
> Be happy anyway.
> The good you do today will often be forgotten,
> Do it anyway.
> Give the best you have and it will never be enough,

Give your best anyway.
In the final analysis it's between you and God.
It was never between you and them anyway.[8]

Here then is more provocative writing on the wall. Read together, as we just did, and its meaning changes, challenging our wider community to look differently at the world.

We've seen writing on the wall through the book of Daniel and through the catacombs; in a few moments we will see it through the bread and wine that we will share together.

---

[8] This prayer may be adapted from a prayer of Keith Kent.

Exodus 28.29–39[1]

MIRIAM SWAFFIELD

'So Aaron shall bear the names of the sons of Israel in the breast piece of judgement on his heart when he goes into the holy place, for a continual remembrance before the Lord.' (Exodus 28.29)

Listen up: love God, love people.

I don't know how good you are at focusing on Jesus when you worship, but my worst story of total distraction during worship happened a few years ago when I was home from 'uni' for Christmas. I'm sitting in our little church next to my younger sister and my mum. Through the church window behind the worship band is a neighbouring house to the church building. Mid-carol, a person appeared in a window of the opposite house. Now it's frosted glass this window, but not quite frosted enough to hide the fact that the next-door neighbour was a middle-aged man enjoying a mid-Christmas-morning shower.

Now, one kind of distraction in church might be your phone buzzing in your pocket, or your tummy rumbling loudly because you didn't eat breakfast. For two girls (I'd like to say I was a teen-ager but embarrassingly this wasn't long ago) sitting next to their mum in church, watching a slightly blurred naked man showering throughout 'In the bleak mid-winter', through the sermon and into 'Hark the herald', this was, quite frankly, game over when it came to focusing on Jesus. We absolutely lost it. By the time we got to the 'Gloooooooria' bit of 'Ding dong merrily on high' we were crying, nay choking, on the giggles. To be fair, I'm pretty

---

[1] This sermon was preached in the context of an 18–30s residential gathering centred on worship interspersed with prayer and talks, with an emphasis on justice and mission.

sure Jesus was too; that was by far the most distracted in worship I have ever been in my life.

I wonder how easy you find it to zone-in to worship, to focus your attention towards loving God, lifting him up despite and above and right in the middle of your circumstances. What have you carried into worship this morning that might be trying to steal your attention from Jesus?

Our generation in general is easily distracted and has grown up in a world of constant diversions: being entertained, targeted and messaged from all angles pretty much all the time. Focused attention in silence, stillness and simplicity is a pretty difficult thing for us.

We carry literal distractions into worship with us, like phones set to vibrate in our pockets – just in case. Perhaps we've been having an argument up until the moment we walked in to worship, or been listening to the charts, or scrolling through the Facebook news feed and so have many different things swirling around our heads, making focusing on Jesus difficult.

Not everything we carry is a superficial distraction, however. Not every distraction can be switched off or turned to aeroplane mode. We have all carried different stories of life and faith into this weekend. We are each carrying a story of God, experiences, hurt, joy, suffering, questions, excitement and doubt as we come together to worship him. Sometimes, what you're carrying into worship isn't something to be ignored but the truthful, raw and real place in which you find yourself. In spite of your circumstances, whether you're buzzing or utterly deflated, we *chose* to worship God anyway, to worship him as a community, whatever the circumstances.

Let me just give you a moment to become aware of yourself. Where you are. How you are. What's in your head. How you're feeling. Just take a breath and attend to yourself. What we carry isn't always a distraction, sometimes it is our fuel for real, honest worship.

Since we all carry things into worship, I want us to notice a way in which we can deliberately choose to pick up and carry something as *part of* our worship and encounter with God. We find an example of this in what might seem a bit of an obscure passage of Scripture in Exodus. So why don't you grab your Bibles, turn them on and get yourselves to Exodus chapter 28, particularly verses 29–30.

This passage comes to us in the middle of chapters describing detailed regulations about the construction of the Temple and the priests' clothes and practices. Earlier in the chapter, there's detail about the priestly garments to be worn to enter into the holy place, the special place of encountering the presence of God. Here we find a description of a breastpiece, worn over the chest, made in rich colours with 12 precious stones fixed onto it, representing the 12 tribes that make up the people of Israel. Each tribe of Israel had their own specific precious stone fixed and displayed on this breastplate.

This short passage in Exodus reveals an approach to worship I have found challenging and helpful. Aaron enters into a place of worship deliberately carrying other people to God. It's not just about Aaron's relationship with God. Aaron represents many others as he worships.

Through the symbolism of the bejewelled breastplate we see Aaron as the high priest, bringing his people before God. This is of course way before Jesus came and became our once and for all high priest, the only one able to bring all people into relationship with God. But Aaron in this passage matters precisely because Jesus became the new Aaron who gives us access to the holy place.

We know Jesus gave us the authority to be priest-like people who can connect others to God too, messengers who reconcile the world to God through him. Because of Jesus, we can all be like Aaron, bringing people into the holy place with God.

Have you ever worshipped like this? When was the last time you deliberately carried other people into the presence of God in worship? Often during worship I will feel prompted to pray for someone or certain situations, but I don't always think of deliberately carrying them into worship from the start, intentionally praying and lifting them before God. Who would you wear over your heart as a constant reminder to love people as you love God, just like Aaron's 12 stones on his breastpiece? Who do you carry to God?

This passage in Exodus reminded me of a story in the New Testament, in Mark 2, of the group of mates bringing their friend who was paralysed to Jesus. Here, in a very literal way, we have another example of the people of God carrying a person in faith to God.

At 'uni' I drew a little prayer mat on an A4 piece of paper with my friends' names written on it, and put it on my wall. In each corner of the paper I wrote the names of other friends, who are followers of Jesus who support me in carrying my friends to meet him.

Who are you carrying to the feet of Jesus in worship, having faith that they can be healed, free, saved, forgiven? And who is alongside you as you carry them? Who are you carrying in your heart as you worship, like wearing the names of your friends on a piece of clothing across your chest, to remind yourself and God of those you want him to encounter?

In carrying other people to God as he worshipped, Aaron was actually showing us a way to live out the two great commandments: to love God and to love neighbour (Mark 12.28–31).The friends carrying the paralysed man on the mat were also showing us a way to live out these commandments.

Listen up family – love God, love people.

That's the instruction to each one of us as individuals, but given to us together as a community. This greatest commandment is given to us as a family, as said by God, written by Moses, modelled by Aaron, underlined again by Jesus Christ and made into a click-through hyperlink to a new reality by the Holy Spirit.

As a community, love God, love people.

We can love God in worship and so bring people before him; like a breastplate that reminds us of the people on our heart and God's. We can carry to God our friends who are weary and burdened, perhaps not yet knowing the life promised in Jesus.

We worship God because he is the only one actually worth worship. We worship God to live out our love for him. We worship God remembering the people he has given us to love in our everyday lives. We cannot love God without loving people and we cannot truly love people without loving God.

So we are back to the question: what are you carrying today? Who are your friends and family close to you who don't know Jesus yet? Who do you carry on your heart, who do you want to bring before God and call his attention to so that their attention might also be caught by him?

Let's take Aaron's example, ultimately embodied by Jesus, and let's be connectors of people to God. As we worship today, I want our mates who aren't here to be on our hearts, just as they are on Jesus'.

Given that we are unlikely to get a breastplate with jewels that represent friends who don't know Jesus yet (despite the possible fashion icons we might become) why not use our hands? Hold out one of your hands and look at your five digits. (Try not to get distracted by the state of your nails.) Can you think of five people you know, five people you share life with who don't follow Jesus? For each digit, name a person, a friend, neighbour, family member, whoever you are reminded of now. Who are your five people you want to bring before God in worship?

What if we started thinking that raising our hands wasn't just about us expressing our vulnerable surrender to God? What if we had our hands in the air to hold up our friends to the Father too? What if every time we came to worship, we remembered that in our hands we carry a representation of our friends whom we want to see saved by Jesus and drawn into worshipping him along with us too?

Let's go into this time of worship now with our friends on our heart.

Let's stand and pray together.

Hold out your hand and hold it up, picture the names and faces of the five people your digits represent.

Place your hand over your heart like Aaron's breastpiece and join with me in agreement as I pray for our mates to come to know Jesus as we carry them with us into worship.

Genesis 1

DAVID WILKINSON

'In the beginning when God created the heavens and the earth, the earth was a formless void and darkness covered the face of the deep, while a wind from God swept over the face of the waters.' (Genesis 1.1–2)

A few years ago I was leading an evening harvest festival service for a small Methodist church. The service was being held in a rather gloomy room where the lights were on. As I began a sermon on Genesis 1, I was conscious that the attention of the congregation was directed a few feet above my head. Glancing up at the light above me I saw the biggest bee I've ever seen. In fact so big that it was casting shadows on me as it circled my head! I paused to try and catch it but the roof was high, the ceiling light was warm and there was no way of reaching it. So starting the sermon again I spent the next 20 minutes trying to preach while this monster insect kept dive-bombing me. All I could do was try and hide behind the Bible I was holding. It was not the most effective of sermons!

In coming to this passage from Genesis, I feel that there are multitudes circling around my head, ready to pounce. Some will be scientists asking whether this old text has anything to say to Big Bang cosmology. Others will be Christians who see a particular interpretation of this chapter as a test of biblical orthodoxy and Christian faith. This controversy has caused Christians to question each other's faith, and great hesitancy to preach on the chapter.

In this there are three important dangers. The first is that it does not recognize that Christians equally committed to the authority of the Bible have followed a number of different interpretations as to the dating of the universe and Genesis 1. The fact that there exist different interpretations should caution us against believing that our interpretation is the only one possible. There needs to be humility that allows us to talk to one another while respecting each other's integrity.

Second, there is a danger of confusing a commitment to biblical authority with a commitment to a particular interpretation of a Bible passage. A commitment to biblical authority encourages us to work harder at a more faithful interpretation of the biblical text, doing justice to its original setting while allowing it to speak into our own setting.

The third danger is much more subtle, yet even more important. The controversy over the dating question often obscures for us the main points of Genesis 1. In the disagreement over the details we lose the very things that the writer, inspired by the Holy Spirit, wants to communicate. Whether the universe was made in seven days a few thousand years ago, or whether it was created over billions of years, is an important question. Yet it is not central to the message of Genesis 1: the overture to the Bible. The scene is being set by introducing some of the fundamental themes that will feature in more detail later in the book. This is an overture about the central character who is introduced in the first verse, and who is central to the close of this overture (Genesis 2.1–3). This is not a passage about the 'how' of creation, nor even primarily about the 'why' of creation. This is a passage about the 'who' of creation. It is an overture that introduces us to the Creator God. So if we 'hide' behind the Bible, what do we learn?

No other creator!

'In the beginning when God created the heavens and the earth' (1.1). The first thing we need to know is that God is the sole creator of the universe. Everything in heaven and earth owes its existence to the sovereign will of God. Now you make a fairly obvious point, can't you give us something more profound? However, it is so important that the writer returns to it a number of times throughout the text, sometimes in subtle ways.

Look, for example, at the first part of verse 16: 'God made the two great lights – the greater light to rule the day and the lesser light to rule the night.' What is the writer referring to? It's fairly clear that the reference is to the sun and the moon, but why are they not called by their respective names? The most probable answer is that in neighbouring cultures they were the names of gods. Genesis 1 seems to be attacking this false theological idea, by saying that they are not gods but simply lights created by the one true God. They are not worthy of worship but simply creations of God. The message conveyed by this text is that God is without peer or competitor; he has no rivals in creation. His word is supreme. He speaks and it is done.

How do we translate this truth that there is no other creator to the world of today? One of the most important applications is in how we view science. Cosmology has allowed us to trace the history of the universe further back in time. Indeed, some scientists such as Stephen Hawking claim that a combination of quantum theory and general relativity will describe the initial conditions of the universe.

Yet, what does this mean? Is quantum theory the creator of the universe? Genesis 1 says a very clear 'no'! Science is extremely successful, but that success is based on the fact that it limits its area of questions. Genesis 1 is reminding us that in terms of questions of meaning and purpose, God is the only answer. Science may describe God's activity in creation, and is to be valued for that. However, we must guard against language that suggests that science is the creator.

The order of faithfulness

The second major theme of Genesis 1 is given not just by the content but also the style. If God gives revelation of his nature in the reality of history, he also does it within various literary styles within the Bible. Here the style reflects a very important truth.

What is striking about the account in the first chapter of Genesis is the pattern and order to God's creation. Much debate between Christians has centred on the seven days, and whether they mean literally seven periods of 24 hours. However, the structure of the seven days reflects a logical rather than chronological order. That is, the first three days deal with shape and the second three with filling up that shape. The structure speaks of the order, harmony and beauty of God's creation. This logical structure does seem to indicate that the aim of the chapter is not meant to be a strict scientific record.

Furthermore, the number seven is not just present in the days. For example, the number of Hebrew words in verse 1 is seven. Verse 2 has 14. Verses 1 to 3 of chapter 2 have 35. The word 'God' occurs 35 times in the chapter, the word 'earth' occurs 21 times, and the phrase 'God saw that it was good' occurs seven times. Now, one does not need to be a great mathematician to see something very subtle is going on. The number seven throughout the Bible is associated with completion, fulfilment and perfection. It speaks of order and goodness.

The style reflects the content, reinforcing the message that the universe is ordered and good because of God. The faithfulness of God is the source of the order in creation.

This too has a very important application to science. Science proceeds on the basis of order in the universe and our ability to discern it. So Christianity, far from being attacked by or attacking science, fundamentally affirms it. God's faithfulness expresses itself in the order of the scientific laws, and that means that science is possible.

Christians have often celebrated such faithfulness in the natural world. Church harvest festivals give thanks to God for the faithfulness of the seasons. It is a truth to celebrate not only in the farming community, but also in the scientific community. The courses of the sun, moon and stars are the result of gravity and, on a greater scale, general relativity. These owe their origin to God. As Kepler said, 'Science is thinking God's thoughts after him.' Those who explore the order of the universe, such as scientists, or those who exploit the order, such as engineers, do so because of God, whether they recognize it or not. In that, science, engineering and technology are Christian ministries.

How can we support those in our congregations who are involved in exploring or using the faithfulness of God in creation? I wonder too if it is reflected in the way that we encourage people to respond to the call of God in their lives. Can we encourage young people and students to study science and delight in thinking God's thoughts after him?

Extravagant diversity

If this talk of order and science gives the idea that God is a boring egghead who can be blamed for numerous students having to learn calculus, we need to notice another over-riding theme in Genesis 1. Alongside the image of lawgiver, king and logician, the Genesis account gives us the picture of God as the great artist.

Here is creativity and diversity in abundance. The earth was formless and empty (v. 2), a phrase that could be translated as 'waste and void'. It is into this monotony, disorder and darkness that God brings differentiation, contrast, structure and order. The acts of separation (vv. 3, 6, 7, 14, 18) give a sense of structure and show God as giving diversity to the created order. Into this structure comes light and life. Once again, here is diversity and creativity. When vegetation is brought forth it is of various kinds, with the ability to reproduce (v. 11). As one child once said to me, 'Wouldn't it have been awful if the only vegetable God created was cabbage!'

Even in the small phrase, 'he also made the stars' (v. 16, NIV), is an awe-inspiring statement of the creativity of God. To a person of the ancient world, the night sky, unpolluted by streetlights, was a myriad of constellations and movement. Today, we are able to see even more. The Hubble Space Telescope and a new generation of ground-based and satellite telescopes have opened up an almost unbelievable vista of diversity. Our sun is a star, a million times larger than the earth. Yet it is only one star in 100 billion stars that make up the Milky Way Galaxy. And the Milky Way Galaxy is only one galaxy in the 100 billion galaxies in the universe.

Why such a universe? People often ask why has God created a Universe with more stars than the grains of sand on the beaches of the world? After all, human life could have arisen with a special creation of one star and one planet. My answer is that the night sky would have been very boring and very few people could have ever done research in theoretical astrophysics! More seriously, the answer is surely in the extravagant diversity of God. God is an artist who creates on a vast canvas with extravagance. He celebrates diversity, making a universe that communicates his greatness, joy and generosity.

In contrast, our delight in greed destroys diversity. It is estimated that there are several million species on the earth, of which possibly less than 10 per cent have been identified. Yet the American scientist Edward Wilson estimates that we as human beings currently wipe out three species every hour. This is due in large part to deforestation, which proceeds at such a rate that an area equivalent to that of the British Isles is being lost every year. In addition, we pollute the land and the sea with persistent pesticides, acid rain and 2 million tonnes of rubbish daily. And then, of course, there are greenhouse gases and global warming.

All because we do not respect the world as God's creation. 'The earth is the LORD's and all that is in it' (Psalm 24.1). There is no other creator. He is the one who gives us the gift of science and technology, but then wants us to use it in a way that celebrates diversity and generosity.

It is blasphemy to destroy the diversity of the world. The extravagance and diversity of the creation reflect the glory of God. In fact, far from being a dry scientific or even theological text, this first chapter of Genesis breathes worship. There are indications that it reflects a liturgical form, that is, it was used in worship. It is neither simple prose nor simple Hebrew poetry but is skilfully arranged. I am more and more convinced that it is a hymn of praise, not to explain the how of creation, but to catch the reader up with the wonder of creation.

For Christians to abuse the environment, or even to spend too much time debating its age, misses the whole point of this passage. So I will continue to 'hide' behind the text, even if the busy bees of a certain interpretation are circling to attack.

But of course there is much more to say. This is just the overture. Soon the plot will speak of the creation of human beings, their sinfulness and a story where this creator of the whole universe reaches out to each one of us in love. But that's for another day.

Homiletic strategies

1 Using an artwork

Jolyon Mitchell works on the interplay between the text and Rembrandt's pictorial interpretation, asking the congregation what they see – what strikes them about the painting? Mitchell points to 'gold' in the picture and to references to gold in the passage and in the wider context of the book of Daniel. Zooming in on Rembrandt, to the golden chain around Belshazzar's neck, he contrasts its apparent solidity with the trembling paleness of the fearful king, explicitly referenced in the text.

The wine spills, the crown slips, and the upward gaze of the characters draws the viewer's eyes. Mitchell applies this visual reading to the biblical text, where Daniel's interpretation of the writing on the wall focuses our attention on the sovereign God.

Riffing around the theme of the writing on the wall, Mitchell offers examples of what this might mean – climate change, resurrection hope and a radically countercultural approach to life. Making Rembrandt available during the sermon offers a visual anchoring point for the variety of themes the preacher is weaving together.

2 Awareness of audience

Miriam Swaffield clearly understands her listeners, giving apposite examples of the distractions that are likely to affect her target audience. She makes references to 'uni', and opens with a personal anecdote likely to amuse her target audience. Perhaps most telling is her request that people turn their Bibles on! Focusing the sermon on the imagined hearer is easier when preaching to a more homogenous congregation, but it is important to ensure there are hooks that will appeal to a range of listeners.

3 Linking the sermon into the context of the whole service

Swaffield deliberately uses Aaron's breastplate as a metaphor of drawing people into worship, allowing her to invite her hearers to use their hands in prayer: each digit to represent a person. The sermon's culminating focus on prayerful hands then allows the move to sung worship.

Whatever follows the sermon, there needs to be space to reflect and, ideally, a relevant bridge into the next stage in the liturgy. This is especially true of sermons that raise painful or thorny issues.

4 Apologetic angle

Apologetics is the art of bringing faith into contemporary conversation – dialogue that is robust, humble and credible. David Wilkinson's sermon demonstrates a powerful apologetic approach. He shows that, in its original context, Genesis 1 engages with other discourses about the nature of divinity, pointing to the Creator God who is without peer. Wilkinson releases the text to do its work in our context, offering a measured apologetic rebuttal of the elevation of science over and against God, seeing science as divine gift. He does this through careful analysis of the content of Genesis 1, without overlooking the theological importance of form. Most notable is his clear communication of the significance of the number 'seven' in the chapter, bringing out a profound sense of the theological creativity of the passage. This points to the perfect creativity of God – science is God's gift; scientific study is a Christian vocation; and care for the environment is a logical expression of commitment to God.

5 Addressing the 'So what?' question

In Wilkinson's sermon, the 'So what?' questions are woven throughout: so why does this text matter and what happens if we distort it? What has the text to say and why should we care? So what difference does this text make to the way we live? Asking and responding to the 'So what?' question pushes the preacher to ask how the strange world of the Bible might reshape our lives.

7

Abrasive

————•◆•————

Loving God,
when we experience Scripture
as painful, and prejudicial,
by the grace of your Spirit
give us courage to look again
without defensiveness.
Lead us to Christ,
we pray.
Amen.

Sometimes the Bible seems like coarse-grain sandpaper abrading our assumptions and perspectives. Some texts cause arms to be folded tight as the hearer sits on their anger, hurt or disbelief; passages that cause the awkward shuffle and the inner question, 'Is this really "the Word of the Lord?"' What are we to make of apparently misogynistic material, texts that seem to have the pastoral sensitivity of a house brick, and Scripture that could be used to endorse bullying regimes in the name of God? The following sermons have much to teach us about working wisely and creatively with such passages.

1 Corinthians 11.1–16

LIS GODDARD

'Be imitators of me, as I am of Christ.' (1 Corinthians 11.1)

Have you ever listened to a muffled conversation through a wall? I'm not going to ask for a show of hands, though I am going to come clean and tell you that, in my misspent youth, I was guilty of such things. That won't be a great surprise to those who know me well! If you have, like me, had such guilty pleasures, you will know that they are very limited – that what you can hear through a wall or floor gives very little away. Your scoping, done this way, tells you very little. You might catch the odd word or phrase, you might hear half-sentences, but you certainly don't get the whole picture. You get a distorted image, and indeed you can often find yourself imagining things that were never said.

If you open the door, go in, and join the conversation, everything changes. And it is the same with our passage today. As so often when we read a snippet from an Epistle, it is a bit like peering through a key hole or listening through the wall. We are in danger of misunderstanding what Paul is saying unless we get the whole picture. We need to open the door on the whole of Paul's thought in 1 Corinthians.

This *is* a really exciting passage, which is pivotal to Paul's thinking. It builds crucially on what has gone before, and to understand it properly we have to see it within that context and in the light of what comes after. If we don't, then we are in danger of thinking – as so many people have – that Paul is a misogynist or that he is confused in his thinking. It is so easy to make up our own conversation, rather than paying attention to the one that Paul has been having – the one that frames these verses.

I wonder what you would say was Paul's most important message in 1 Corinthians. Perhaps something about love? Or the gifts?

Both of those are important but both are laced through with one key message that is there throughout the letter. It is summed up in 1 Corinthians 10.33: 'I try to please everyone in everything I do, not seeking my own advantage, but that of many, so that they may be saved.' Paul speaks again and again in the run-up to our passage about freedom – his own freedom, the freedom of the believer, and the fact that we shouldn't stand on our rights, or shout about our abilities, but always think about how who we are and what we do relates to others.

Paul writes in 1 Corinthians 9.19: 'For though I am free with respect to all, I have made myself a slave to all, so that I might win more of them.' It is within this context that we come to 1 Corinthians 11. We discover that it begins not with confusing language about the 'head', language that seems to keep changing its meaning, but with Paul's injunction, very like that in Philippians 2, 'Be imitators of me, as I am of Christ.' Our Bibles put a section break there, but of course these are extra-biblical. Paul would have known nothing of such an arrangement of his text. Verses 1 and 2 flow one into the next. For Paul, following the example of Christ links directly to what it means to live in the way that the rest of the chapter exhorts us to. So what does that look like?

One of the fairy stories that I really couldn't get on with as a child was that of the Emperor's new clothes. I just couldn't understand, no matter how often I heard it, how anyone could be that gullible – or indeed how his subjects could go along with the myth that he was wearing a fine suit when in fact he was as naked as the day he was born. I remember clearly thinking, 'No one would really behave like that. They would just say it as it is. They wouldn't just believe a lie like that, would they?'

And yet – and yet – we know in our own world how easily things get redefined and then how very easily it seems that people believe something they would never previously have believed. Think only of what is going on today surrounding sex and gender. These are things we can individually define for ourselves. We are being told we can no longer speak in terms of male and female or of the difference between them, because all difference is simply culturally conditioned. Bizarrely, two thousand years ago this was the precise issue Paul was addressing within the early Church, but coming from a very different angle. Men and women had suddenly discovered overwhelming freedom in Christ, the freedom of redemption – the freedom that Paul himself had spoken of in Galatians 3.28: 'There is no longer Jew or Greek, there is no longer slave or free, there is no longer male and female; for all of you are one in Christ Jesus.' They had suddenly discovered the freedom of the New Creation, the freedom that meant that the old ways were finished and redemption had come. What they hadn't realized was that, in this New Creation, the mutuality that was God's original intention between male and female in creation was restored. Earlier in 1 Corinthians Paul had written one of the most radical lines anywhere in Scripture about male–female relations: 'the wife does not have authority over her own body, but the husband does; likewise the husband does not have authority over his own body, but the wife does' (1 Corinthians 7.4). To speak at that time of this mutual authority and yielding between husband and wife was absolutely radical.

Alongside this, women were discovering the freedom to pray and prophesy in mixed congregations, and Paul is clear that this was totally right and acceptable. But they were losing control – boy were they enjoying themselves. We've already seen earlier in Corinthians that there were all sorts of issues about a lack of sexual inhibitions. Now here we discover that they have forgotten what it means to live with sexual differentiation. For them it wasn't so much multiple genders as no gender differentiation – because suddenly they were free, free from the constraints that differentiation had placed on them for so long.

The women were literally 'letting their hair down'; in a culture where it was considered so shameful that to do so in the streets could be cited as the reason for divorce. Paul is calling both men and women back to remembering that, although they are now free, and creation has been restored, that does not mean the end of sexual differentiation. Rather it means the fulfilling of creation as it was always meant to be. So, in salvation terms, there is no differentiation between male and female: both are saved by Christ's work. But in creation they are the same but different. They are both made in the image of God. Man is the glory of God, in the sense that he is the culmination of creation. And woman is the glory of man. That does not mean that woman is somehow less than man. To speak of her as man's glory is to speak of her in some sense completing him, because 'It is not good for the man to be alone', hence the man's response to her: 'This at last is bone of my bones and flesh of my flesh' (Genesis 2.23) – one flesh, one body, one image. Paul tells us 'neither was man created for the sake of woman, but woman for the sake of man'. This echoes Paul's language in 2 Corinthians 8.9 when he writes, 'For you know the generous act of our Lord Jesus Christ, that though he was rich, yet for your sakes he became poor, so that by his poverty you might become rich.' This points us to the clear mutuality intended in this passage. Adam was the one who needed help, who was incomplete on his own, and God gave him the woman who was his glory to minister to him, to be his helper 'for his sake'.

This is a remarkable passage, because here Paul expounds what it means for us to have been made as interdependent sexual people, something that our culture often finds hard to accept. There is no doubt that it matters that we are sexually differentiated, male and female, and that in some sense this images the interdependent differentiated relationships of the Trinity.

What Paul wants for the Corinthians, as indeed for each of us, is what he keeps on saying throughout this remarkable book. He wants them to learn to value not only their own freedom in Christ but also that of others. He wants them to listen to the whole conversation, to join in the conversation that the Trinity shares. He wants them to step into the fullness that God has for men and women, remembering their createdness, and not distorting it or the glory of creation seen in maleness and femaleness.

I wonder how much we listen at keyholes to distorted conversations. Or allow our perception to be distorted by Chinese whispers, by what other people tell us is the reality? Instead, shouldn't we be joining in the conversation of mutuality God wants to have with us, that he wants us to model as male and female to his broken world? God's word to us today is: don't be scared. Be the man, be the woman he has made you to be.

Step out into the leadership and challenge he has prepared for us – together.

Mark 10.2–16

MARK TANNER

'Some Pharisees came, and to test him they asked, "Is it lawful for a man to divorce his wife?"' (Mark 10.2)

Welcome to the topsy-turvy world of Mark's Gospel. Let's be honest: sometimes texts like this just seem embarrassing. What would your friends say? How would the media interpret this? Who is more out of touch – Jesus, or the disciples? I mean . . . the disciples . . . what kind of idiots are they? Don't they appreciate a child's sanctity? How can they turn angels away? If you want innocence, look at a sleeping baby! Kids might get into scrapes, but if anyone's pure, they are! At least Jesus gets this right – children can come to him any time, the kingdom of God belongs to them!

But his teaching on divorce . . . clearly *he* never attended pastoral training at Cranmer Hall. Of course marital break-up isn't ideal, but does he really think labelling divorcees adulterers is going to help? Get real! Divorce happens . . . and people have enough problems with guilt . . .

. . . buuut . . . this is Jesus . . . can I even say this?

Agghhh – it is confusing! I'm overplaying my hand trying to grasp how we feel, but I don't really want to argue that kids are perfect or that divorce is good.

I want to come to Scripture with open eyes, a humble heart and a genuine desire to hear God and understand what the text says . . . holding everything else I know of life wisely and gently. Sometimes this feels like the intellectual and moral equivalent of being stuck in an oversized washing machine: the world is spinning and I'm not sure which way is up!

When you start scuba diving you learn stuff that seems obvious but is vitally important. Like: bubbles always go up! To the surface, follow the bubbles! It's obvious, why stress it? Because of something called nitrogen narcosis. When you are underwater, the gasses in your air supply do odd things to you. Seventy-nine per cent of air is nitrogen. We don't notice it because it has no effect on us normally, but deep down, under pressure, it behaves like alcohol. At some point you get drunk on nitrogen . . . it's called 'getting narked'. When you are seriously narked, just as when you are drunk, you lose judgement. Divers have died because they literally didn't know which way was up. They swam deeper because the bubbles seemed wrong. Divers who have been dragged to safety report their confusion that the bubbles started going down!

Except they didn't!

Bubbles go up!

If you think a bubble is going down, you are narked; you have lost your grip on reality, and you are in mortal danger. We need alarm bells like this when we start losing our grip.

It is a good thing we have such a tight grip on reality when we deal with the issues in this passage! In our post-Freudian, post-industrial, post-sexual revolution, post-Savile world, we *know* that sex is an inalienable right, we *know* that children are innocent, sacred and to be prioritized. We *know* that guilt is unhelpful, religious rules are oppressive, and if we follow modern wisdom we *can* construct a better world than our forebears . . . so watch the relational bubbles and get with the times! Look at the effect our teaching has, the fruit our choices produce, watch the bubbles . . .

. . . here's a bubble, look, it's that kid down the street! Actually, that's odd . . . but this *must be* an exception, surely there's a reason they appear selfish . . .

. . . here's another: oh . . . well, she's clearly better out of the marriage; I do hope her claims of happiness aren't as hollow as they sound . . .

. . . another: no, not that one, they're from a broken home . . .

. . . another: no, he had a bad role model . . .

. . . no, not that one, that's bullying . . . abuse, jealously, hatred . . .

Bubble, bubble, bubble . . . the world's gone mad . . . the bubbles aren't going up . . .

. . . or maybe we have lost our frame of reference. Maybe the world is disorientated and lost without Christ.

Jesus' words can appear hard, but without him life's bubbles cry out their warnings. This is no surprise given who Jesus is. Here is the Lord of life and love, speaking truth and grace even when it's tough . . . and if we can but hear, life comes back into view . . . bubbles are meant to go up . . . the surface is near. Let's look again: the religious leaders come to test Jesus – this is the same word we ask to be rescued from in the Lord's Prayer when we pray, 'lead us not into temptation (or testing)'. Here is a hard question designed to catch him out, and to answer it Jesus reaches back to the very start of creation. 'Is divorce OK with God?' they ask. 'God never intended it,' he answers.

Human beings were created in the image of the One who is love itself; we're made for faithful love, for eternal love; for transforming, patient, kind, thoughtful, fulfilling love. Yes, we are broken, but God's image lives on in the fundamental building blocks of who you are. The image of God is marred but clearly present. God is ignored, even shunned, but his primal invitation of love resounds on every continent and in every heart. 'Till death us do part' as two lives join in the radically prophetic step of holy matrimony, means 'till death us do part', because that is what it is to love . . . no mere emotion, no pursuit of gratification, or search for security: marriage reflects the image of God. Divorce is a breaking of this image. It is a tearing apart of that which God has joined together . . . and deep down we recognize this. What child hopes to get divorced? Who walks up the aisle dreaming that this is the first step towards a glorious separation? That's nonsense. Divorce is horrible. It breaks lives and wounds hearts.

Yes, it happens, and sometimes it is the least worst option. There are more and less innocent parties. But let's not pretend that it is good . . . or that bubbles sink . . . this is to lose our eternal frame of reference.

And Jesus goes further. Later, when his disciples ask, he teaches that remarriage is adultery. Bear with me if this hurts . . . but Jesus gently and simply speaks truth, knowing that this is the only way to deal with brokenness. We don't fix problems by ignoring them, and this is the heart of Jesus' message. Today we so often deal with brokenness, or sin as the Bible calls it, by saying that it's not our fault and it doesn't matter. Jesus doesn't do that. He looks sin in the eye and offers a radical alternative – forgiveness. He recognizes that brokenness is brokenness and that, left unaddressed, it will be the death of us. It doesn't matter where the fault lies; what matters is that we are ensnared, ignoring the bubbles and heading downwards. Pretending the surface is just below us doesn't make it so . . . only the radical truth that we are disoriented, lost and in need of a saviour deals with our peril.

Sin needs forgiveness . . . just as a broken leg needs setting, not exercise. We don't remove the pain of divorce by saying it doesn't matter, or regulating it with a religious code. Jesus' radical alternative is that we come to God in humility like a child. This passage is not about childlike perfection or innocence; it can't be, because they aren't. Children are notable because they can accept correction and still know they are loved. It's how they learn when they are small, and the text is clear it is *little children* who are being brought. Children know they get things muddled up, they mess up, they don't know who started the argument . . . but Mum can sort it. The football has broken the window and they can't fix it. The kingdom of God belongs to such as these.

The question, you see, is not whether you are an adulterer, it is whether you are forgiven; just as it's not whether you are a liar, a cheat, acquainted with envy, lust, greed or anger . . . in Christ *all* can be made new.

Divorce is terrible. That is not to point the finger at those who find themselves there, it is just to recognize that it's horrible. Let's name it, and in everything let's learn to come as little children. It's hard, it's real, but the cross changes even this . . . that's the power of Jesus' forgiveness, his new life. The light at the surface looms, hope dawns.

And don't think it's just those who are divorced in the spotlight. This is Jesus' offer for each of us in our muddled complexity . . . we are caught in a whirlpool that cannot be sorted by the values of this world. We are broken, trapped, disorientated and lost. It's hard, it's real, but coming to Christ with a child's humility begins to change everything . . . it is rarely easy, but it is eternally real . . . And in this place . . . of honesty, humility, and trembling hope . . . Jesus offers healing, hope, redemption.

It's still hard, but you are not alone and the surface is near.

Romans 13.1–7

LINDSEY GOODHEW

'Let every person be subject to the governing authorities; for there is no authority except from God, and those authorities that exist have been instituted by God.' (Romans 13.1)

I was advised to begin with a political joke, to lighten the mood. Yet, trawling the Internet, I didn't find anything particularly funny or comfortable in the telling. The only one that raised so much as a smile was this one-liner, about the American President George Bush: 'The last time anyone listened to a bush, a bunch of people ended up in the desert for 40 years.'

What I did find were unpleasant jibes masquerading as humour. Political jokes and satirical quiz shows reflect what countless public polls have been telling us for years, that when it comes to trust and respect, politicians come pretty low down. In 1983, 18 per cent of us trusted politicians to tell the truth; in 2009, in the wake of the expenses scandal, this dropped to just 13 per cent – even lower than for journalists. We can debate whether or not this mistrust is merited. But I mention this simply to suggest that such – at best – pervasive ambivalence or – at worst – outright hostility to those in authority, runs in stark contrast to Paul's apparently ringing endorsement in Romans 13.

On the surface, Paul's meaning seems pretty clear; yet I'm sure I'm not the only one who, on first reading or hearing these words, wants to shout out: 'But, But, But . . .'.

But what about evil regimes and corrupt government, new and old – the Caligulas, Herods and Neros; the Hitlers, Stalins and Saddams: surely Paul can't mean that each one was personally appointed by God, their authority in no circumstances to be resisted? Let's dig a bit deeper into the passage and cross-reference it with the wider biblical perspective to find out more.

When Paul speaks of 'governing authorities' he is talking in broader terms than modern-day assemblies and governments – they include the civil authorities, those entrusted with the task of governing, collecting taxes and enforcing the rule of law. In contemporary terms this means judges, civil servants, as well as politicians and those in government. And we must remind ourselves that Paul writes as one who has suffered at the hands of the very authorities he is commending his listeners to honour and respect. As a citizen of Rome he knows a lot about a governing authority that, while arguably one of the most successful and civilizing empires in history, was also one of the most brutal. Paul is talking about a very non-Christian government – a pagan empire. The authorities Paul has in view were at best unfriendly and at worst actively hostile towards the church.

For the writer Tim Keller, an increasingly secular West is only just beginning to experience the level of hostility that first-century believers faced, with the twenty-first-century persecuted Church experiencing it every day. Yet it is this type of state that Paul calls Christians to submit themselves to. Paul's words are not those of an unquestioning citizen, one who kept his head down, never rubbing up against the authorities; but rather those of a follower of Jesus – the one who felt the full crucifying force of Roman law.

Certainly this passage has been used to support oppressive regimes. Michael Cassidy, the founder of African Enterprise, recalls meeting the then South African President P. W. Botha in October 1985, the time of the National Initiative for Reconciliation. Michael Cassidy had hoped for signs of repentance, with assurances from the President that apartheid would be dismantled. Instead Botha began the interview by reading him these opening verses of Romans 13, clearly imagining that this passage was enough to justify unequivocal support of the government's current policy.

So, must we conclude that Paul is giving unqualified endorsement to those who govern, or are there any hints within the passage that this support has limits?

The first hint comes in the choice of the word 'be subject' in verse 1. 'Let every person be subject to the governing authorities.' Paul calls Christians to be subject, to submit, rather than to obey. To be subject recognizes our place in an ordered society – by which I don't mean the Downton Abbey type of order; rather the positive structures that enable society to function for the greater good of all. It acknowledges that as a general rule certain people or institutions have authority over us – be they teachers, scout leaders, our boss, the rule of law – for positive reasons. In general, such submission will mean obedience to what governing authorities tell us to do. At its simplest, obedience of pupil to teacher is important as it creates a positive environment in which all children have the opportunity to learn and fulfil their potential. But, as one commentator notes, submission to government may be compatible with disobedience to government in certain exceptional circumstances. In the hierarchy of relations, God is after all the head; and all subordinate submissions must always be measured in relationship to our all-embracing submission to him.

The second hint comes in verses 3 and 4: 'For rulers are not a terror to good conduct, but to bad . . . for it [their authority] is God's servant for your good.' Paul asserts that those in authority are 'God's servants' (repeated in verse 6) who ensure that the right and good thing is done. Governing authorities are part of God's plan. They are necessary in a fallen world to promote justice – enforcing right and wrong – to ensure the good ordering of society, with an authority derived from God's authority. Remember Jesus' words to Pilate, 'You would have no power over me unless it had been given you from above' (John 19.11). Pilate misused his authority to condemn Jesus – but the authority he used had been delegated to him by God.

As God's servants those in authority must operate within God's law and good purposes. They are not free to do whatever they wish – and our submission to such authorities is shaped by the ways such authorities fulfil their God-given calling. This begs a bigger question – how do we judge when those in authority have either overstepped the mark, or failed to live up to their responsibilities? And what actions might we legitimately take? A question for another time.

The third and final hint that there are limits to our support of those in authority comes in verse 7: 'Pay to all what is due to them' – taxes, revenue, respect, honour. Paul clearly echoes Jesus' teaching, 'Give to Caesar what is Caesar's and to God what is God's.' Here Jesus undercuts the belief that the king or emperor had divine authority: 'yes' to taxes but 'no' to worship. This understanding went deep into the consciousness of the early Church, where Christians risked great danger as they acknowledged an authority higher than the emperor, where Jesus – not Caesar – is Lord. These hints from the passage suggest that, far from advocating an uncritical acceptance of established governing authority, there are times when such authorities must be resisted – there is a limit to their power. Such hints and the conclusions are supported elsewhere in Scripture, for example by Daniel and his three friends in their refusal to obey a Babylonian king. And by the apostles who, when ordered by the governing authorities to stop preaching the good news, reply, 'We must obey God rather than any human authority' (Acts 5.29).

So what can we take away from this passage?

First, Romans 13 encourages us to enlarge our vision of God, for what underpins this passage is a deep conviction in the supreme sovereignty of God. Ultimately, for Paul, God is in control of the whole of life, working his purpose out in every aspect – including the political; working his purposes out in those who recognize him and call him Lord, and through those who do not. Think of Cyrus in Isaiah, of Nebuchadnezzar in Daniel – both rulers who did not recognize the God of Israel and yet who God worked through for his sovereign purpose.

Second, Romans 13 affirms the positive role of governing authorities in God's good purposes for us all. We are called to support, respect and to pray (see 1 Timothy) for all those who carry the burden of office – be it local or national government, those in our judicial system and courts, or civil servants. We might ask ourselves about our own attitudes to those in authority – do we tend to have too high or too low a view of the authorities God has established over us? Romans 13 also encourages us to get involved – by which I mean not just being politically aware but actively considering careers in government and the legal system.

Third and finally, Romans 13 reminds us that a sound reading of the Bible requires us to read across Scripture and not put undue weight on one isolated verse or passage. When P. W. Botha quoted Romans 13 to Michael Cassidy he failed to do so in the light of the rest of Scripture or the context of Paul's life. In putting Romans 13 into the wider context of Scripture we too are asked to consider how and where we might be called to challenge authority in order to obey God. For, as the Apostle Peter proclaimed in Acts chapter 5, our ultimate allegiance is not to any governing authority, but to God alone.

Homiletic strategies

1 Bookending with extended imagery

Both Lis Goddard and Mark Tanner introduce an image that extends through their respective sermons, holding the structure together, emerging at the end to give a satisfying sense of completion. Goddard begins with the image of overhearing a conversation in another room, allowing her to raise the idea of distorted understanding. She invites us through the doorway and into the conversation, allowing her to unpack how the passage has been framed, helping us to hear Paul's theological intent. She ends with the image of listening in at doorways, using this as a metaphor for passively relying on half-heard messages, rather than actively engaging with God.

Tanner introduces his diving illustration early in the sermon and weaves the bubble imagery throughout, using the idea of a 'narked' diver (who sees bubbles as falling) as a sign of our disorientation apart from Christ, our true frame of reference. Ending with a picture of the hearer as a diver about to break through the surface of the water to safety, he offers the implicit image of Jesus as a diving buddy.

2 Addressing the problem

All three sermons address the problems the respective texts present to us. Goddard explores Pauline thinking in relation to gender relations, asking the hearer not to write off Paul as a misogynist, but to listen again. Tanner says at the outset it 'just seems embarrassing'. This technique communicates to the listener that the preacher has taken the text, and its challenge, seriously. Lindsey Goodhew raises the congregational objection and addresses it in the section following 'But, But, But . . .'. Her response involves close textual analysis, as well as setting the text within the wider context

123

of Scripture, offering biblical hints to support the thesis that authority has its limits.

Tanner's text from Mark 10 presents the temptation to skip over difficult teaching around divorce to focus on more congenial material, where little children come to Jesus. But to leave the divorce teaching hanging in the air is like the bad smell no one dares to mention. By naming the difficulty up front Tanner can address it in a way that is pastorally astute, and offers genuine grace, rather than the cheap variety.

3 The double helix of text and context

Imagine a double helix: one strand is called 'text' and the other 'context'. This helix can be seen in Goodhew's sermon. She begins firmly rooted in the contemporary context, with humorous reference to George Bush, mention of polls showing how little we trust politicians, and acknowledgement of a wide range of corrupt regimes. This context strand corkscrews through the sermon with reference to Tim Keller, Michael Cassidy and President P. W. Botha, a call to consider careers in the legislature or the judiciary, with a final reference to Cassidy and Botha.

The text strand references Paul's understanding and experience of 'governing authorities', and then more detailed focus on the verses in hand, with reference to wider biblical texts, enabling Goodhew to offer three clear take-home points from the passage. This double helix communicates that the biblical passage speaks into the contemporary context.

Part 3

WRESTLING WITH
THE WORD

8

An Archbishop's sermon: Acts 1.1–11; Luke 24.44–53[1]

JUSTIN WELBY

'In the first book, Theophilus, I wrote about all that Jesus did and taught from the beginning.' (Acts 1.1)

Ascension is about power and victory, but not as we know it. If you're a fan of *Star Trek* you'll hear the allusion: 'It's life, Jim, but not as we know it.' Though I'm told no one ever actually said that, any more than Sherlock Holmes said, 'Elementary, my dear Watson.' But even though I am not a Trekkie it's a good line.

Ascension is about power or victory, but not as we know it. The accounts include words like 'power', 'kingdom', 'witness', 'proofs' and 'promise of the Father' – such that the disciples, who weren't any quicker on the uptake after the resurrection than before, ask about the restoration of the kingdom of Israel. If *power* is going to be given to them surely that means conquest? If Jesus speaks of a *kingdom* surely they are about to see it? Given the *proof* that he has overcome death, are they themselves the *witnesses* – the honoured heralds, sent in the name of the Lord?

No, it is not as we know it. The power is intangible and does not make us Superman or Wonder Woman. The kingdom is elusive and invisible. The *proofs* and *promises* will be disbelieved by many. The victory offers no conclusive culmination, only a

---

[1] Ascension Day Eucharist, St Martin-in-the-Fields, London, 14 May 2015. Reproduced by permission.

beginning; while being a witness invites danger, leading to sacrifice and suffering, if not death.

The power that comes is to be given away not hung on to; Jesus was no Mugabe clinging to power. There would be no public glory or acclaim, merely hard work and sacrifice, like most of those who serve the Church round the world today. I spoke to someone yesterday working for reconciliation in a civil war, whose name will never be known outside the circles of his own friends – yet he carries a cross of suffering for Christ. Put like that it makes the worst of any recent party manifesto look like words of gold, to which people would flock by contrast. Few would be elected on the manifesto of Jesus, surely?

Yet the Church grew at such a rate, despite opposition and suffering, that 300 years later the Empire that had casually swiped away the life of Jesus with the sort of attention we might give to a mosquito, found itself honouring and converting to the faith. The same disciples who beforehand seem foolish and act only in their own interests, were willing to lay down their lives, confident in the promises of God, the kingdom of God and the triumph of Christ.

The Ascension *is* victory, power and life, but not as we know it. So what do we know, and where is our confidence? The outcome of the completed victory of Jesus is that Christians cannot live enmeshed in the same concerns and despairs and joys any longer. The result of the completed victory of Jesus is that in all history there is only one inevitability: the promised return of Jesus the Christ. He will come back in just the way he departed, when the kingdom of heaven will be fully visible and tangible. No setbacks, no failures of the visible Church, or its leaders; no powers on earth or in heaven are able to cause history to have any other conclusion. Jesus has established the way ahead.

Yet the path often does not feel inevitably leading to a glorious conclusion. The conquest of evil does not look definitive. The Christian path is a path of suffering because the path of Jesus was a path of suffering – and his followers cannot expect a better time than he had. Not miserable and dour suffering, but a path that is full of the presence of Christ even if also the presence of evil. He has gone and we are to carry on, filled with the Holy Spirit, but carry on notwithstanding.

We are surely more than ever aware of the suffering not only of Christians but of all sorts and kinds of people, more than we ever have been. Their images, their agonies, come to us direct, unmediated, calling loudly. Yet it should not be a path of solitary suffering, because the Church is a family of witnesses to the reality of Jesus. Suffering is amplified by isolation and healed by association.

One visit abroad I made last year was so short that if you had blinked you would have missed it. Yet the local bishop, in a country afflicted with Ebola, spoke of the effect of us being there. Why? Because it told him he was not alone. The path of suffering is also one where the church family is empowered by the Holy Spirit of God. The Holy Spirit does not give us the power to fight, to attack each other, to hate, to destroy – but the power to love, to witness, to declare repentance for those things that destroy life and forgiveness; a power that liberates us to a new future.

Last Sunday we remembered 70 years since VE day. At the service in Westminster Abbey was a bishop from Germany. That country has demonstrated repentance and has found renewal and forgiveness, and thus Europe has been given the light of reconciliation and the hope of peace. That is a sign of the work of the Spirit through human beings.

What could be more important than the message Jesus' followers are left to proclaim? What can be more essential to that message than the gift of power from God; power to liberate not dominate, to bring life not law, freedom not fear? Ascension is about power or victory, but not as we know it. The Ascension set our destination, and in its compelling conquest assures us of the promises and mission that catch hold of us and compel us to change our world; never to despair, always to endure, to rejoice, to celebrate, to tolerate our failings, patiently to endure suffering – knowing that the victory of Jesus the Christ is certain.

Jesus brought us God – but not as we know it. Our challenge is not to make Jesus fit the God we know, but to realize that God is the Jesus we see.

9

A last sermon: Colossians 1.15–22; Luke 13.10–17[1]

RUTH ETCHELLS

'He is the image of the invisible God, the firstborn of all creation.' (Colossians 1.15)

Listening to or watching the news coming out of Egypt, and the huge number of individual interviews from the crowds, one word has been used repeatedly: *'Freedom! We want freedom.'* It is a cry as old, I suspect, as the oldest human social structure, and for Christians such a cry coming from the streets of Egypt has a particular poignancy, echoing as it does the cry of hundreds of centuries ago, articulated by Moses, 'Set my people free!'

When I chose the readings for tonight, several months ago, I had no idea they would have such immediate political relevance. For of course in the end both of them are about freedom. I was simply asked to choose a reading or readings important in my own journey of faith. And with very little hesitation I chose the marvellous passage we've heard, from the first chapter of Colossians: one of the most far-reaching statements of faith in the whole Bible, and certainly one of the greatest hymns. And I chose the Gospel reading, of the healing of the disabled woman, as an illustration of what that great statement in Colossians is fundamentally about.

Just remind yourselves of that Lucan reading now. It's a simple story: Jesus is in the synagogue on the Sabbath attending regular

---

[1] St John's College, Durham, Eucharist, 8 February 2011. Reproduced by permission.

131

worship. He notes the disabled woman, he has heard her story, and knows the length of her suffering; and so he acts out a parable. He calls her out and he heals her. From being bent double, for the first time in 18 years she straightens up: a deeply dramatic moment. And what is the first thing she does? She praises God.

Now wouldn't you think that a spontaneous outburst of praise to God would rejoice the heart of a religious leader? *Shouldn't it have done?* Instead, we're told, the ruler of the synagogue – presiding minister, if you like – is really angry, and gives the people (not Jesus, note, but the people) a thorough telling off for desecrating the Sabbath, the holy day, by coming to look for healing.

Wrong expectation, he thought. For you see, those religious leaders truly thought they'd got holiness taped. Measured out, contained, *protected* with a set of rules and rituals that were meant to safeguard the people from unintended blasphemy, meant to keep them mindful of the Unknowable and Sovereign God into whose presence they'd come. The intention behind the regulations and rituals was wholly admirable. But somewhere along the road they had lost sight of the glory of loving-kindness that is the true nature of divine holiness. And by his provocative action Jesus was reminding them of it. They had lost sight of what the religious rules were really about: God's will to free humanity from all that threatens our good – 'Satan's bondage' – as the story puts it.

Dietrich Bonhoeffer once spoke of the sinfulness of stupidity. Not the stupidity of being no good at sums – or even essay writing; or, as in my own case, being hopelessly illiterate when it comes to computers. He was speaking of spiritual and moral stupidity, of somehow inwardly blocking out, not seeing, the unshakeable and profound and mind-blowing divine laws of life itself, and the kind of living involved in them. And so often the reason for this self-imposed blindness is that we have this terrible tendency to project on God our own image, and remake him in it, instead of the other way round. And when we do, he is *always, always* too small.

And that's why I've chosen these two readings. Because they're both about the gospel as freeing us from every kind of bondage, and two kinds especially. First, the powerful bondage of hopelessness or even despair, in the face of sickness and suffering; or events that cripple us emotionally; or traumatic natural disasters; or the mystery of evil abroad in the world in human desire for power, or greed, or sadism, or simply weak human selfishness, or even simple lack of imagination, which is a sort of stupidity. And the second kind of bondage is that which we impose on ourselves (and often on those around us): from what it's 'all right' or 'not all right' to wear, to eat or drink, to the much bigger issues of the right and wrong ordering of our lives. In the past, for instance, such questions as white marrying black, Muslim marrying Christian . . . and so, sadly, sometimes to an absolute prescriptiveness about how we should worship God or even name him. And the horror of religious pogroms have all begun here.

In this Gospel Jesus is dealing with both kinds of bondage: the hopelessness that can attend human sickness and suffering; and the legalistic bondage of the religious Thought Police. For the Sabbath was indeed the day to worship the most holy God; but 'holiness' is actually the shining dazzle of divine love exchanged continually within the Trinity and poured out for creation in all its forms, for our deepest and most joyful good. And so, Christ is saying, how *can* you, on this day specially given to thanking God for his deep purposes of love, how *can* you cross the divine loving intent for this woman by imposing your own bondage, of when God might be allowed to heal and when he mustn't? (And the frightening thing is that in some form or another we often still do it.)

So to the great passage of Colossians 1. Paul wrote this letter to them because he could see the unity of their little community was at risk, from two directions. On the one hand from some such religious perfectionism as Christ deals with in the Luke story. (In our own day it can range from over-prescriptiveness about liturgical dress, gesture or phrase, to what songs, choruses, hymns are 'OK'.

133

Or even, in some parts of the Church, what gender we're offering.) The other threat was from those pressing a de-personalized abstraction of the gospel, turning it into a worldly and empty rationalized philosophy; deliberately emptying it of the marvellous, which is inherently its nature. (Again, in our own day, there's a lot of it about . . .)

And so, in this great statement of our faith, we are brought to the core gospel, in an ever-expanding vision that takes our breath away, of who Jesus actually is: Lord of all that exists, seen or not seen. And in the kind of Lordship he exercises: for every speculation of humanity, every glimpse of the infinity of space, every mind-blowing discovery of scientists and technologists, every dream of artists, every wondering discovery of the heart-stopping beauty of our earth and its creatures, every amazed experience of the tenderness of another's love – all that shapes our ultimate horizons, emotional, intellectual, aesthetic, physical – all our 'beyonds' are left behind in this glimpse of who and what we worship in the Lord Jesus Christ.

If tonight we can catch again, however briefly, just a glimpse of the scale of what we are caught up in and the Being we might be handing our lives over to, then it could transform our whole perspective on the dailyness of our living, from the minor irritation of other people's habits to the big things like fear of failure, or anxiety about 'A' or 'B' whom I love but can't seem to get it right, or how to shift the huge workload. Or how to cope with my muddle about what I believe, or even if I believe anything at all. Or how to face those who sneer at my Christian faith as old-fashioned, childish, even naive. Getting away from the God who's too small to the God who is bigger than I can cope with is the first breakthrough. For it's when our God is too small that our faith cracks. It's when our God is too petty that we lose our capacity for wonder.

Here's how Veronica Zundel,[2] lovely Christian twentieth-century poet, puts it:

---

[2] Zundel, V., 'Song', in *Faith in Her Words*. Lion Publishing, Oxford, 1991; reproduced with permission. The full poem appear on p. 139.

I scan you on the figured page
in tales of every distant age
and chant you in a holy song
but yet I hear, I see you wrong

I am so small
you are so all

. . .

[for] narrow is my inward sight
I do not spell your meanings right
and guttering my outward gaze
I do not steady trace your ways

my steps are small
to map your all

then break me wide your raging word
in flintstruck light from darkness stirred
and break me wide your dancing love
that soars the hawk, that swoops the dove

I am so small
you are so all in all.

For here's the challenge: when you are speaking of Christ, Paul says, when you have begun to know him, really turn to look at him, you are encountering the One who is the direct image of the most holy and unseen God. The First Letter of John puts it clearly and simply:

What we have heard, what we have seen with our eyes, what we have looked at and touched with our hands – this life was revealed, and we have seen it and testify to it, and declare to you the eternal life that was with the Father and was revealed to us. (1 John 1.1–2)

He shows us *God*, who is Creator of all that was and is and ever will be.
And in him – in Jesus – a marvellous phrase, 'all things hold to-gether'. That is, he's like a force of gravity, holding together all the

forces of life. For he is Lord not only of the Jewish people, not only of his own followers, but of *the world.* Correction: of the *worlds.* Not of this world only, but through space and time, all the conceivable and *in*conceivable universes in every space/time dimension in which they may or could exist. Lord too of their inhabitants, whether they're Little Green Men from Mars, or *Dr Who* specials, or our own earth still teeming with creatures including ourselves. Lord also of heavenly beings of infinite regions. For our Lord Jesus is not simply the *sum* of everything but the *beyond* of everything.

And all that was put to our service: so that through his intervention in our alienated human life, all things 'in heaven and on earth' are reconciled with God . . . and so in the end with each other.

It's not surprising that we find it difficult to lasso such tremendous notions within our own thought patterns. John Pritchard once put it like this:

> We're bound to misunderstand what God is like. Any description we come up with is like trying to play a Beethoven symphony on a tin whistle. We don't have the instruments for it. We don't have the language. It's like asking a child in a nursery school what a university is like.[3]

And so, trying to fit him into our picture of things, we're like the little girl of whom he tells:

> I was talking to a group of children about God. 'How old is He?' one asked.
>
> 'Very old', I said. 'A million years?' 'More than that', I said. 'He's always been alive.' One little girl thought about this for a while and then she announced sternly, 'He must need a bath soon!'

Out of the mouths . . . perhaps it's we who need the bath – an eye-bath – to glimpse him for what he truly is. And it's why the immediate and tender presence of Jesus here among us is the way for us to grasp the extraordinary divine love seeking us out in our

---

[3] Pritchard, J. P., *How to Explain your Faith.* SPCK, London, 2006, p. 53.

need. Because God, the 'unseen', 'beyond us' God, is the sort of God Jesus shows him to be. Because he's both vast enough and involved enough. Because he joined us in all the mess, and transformed our future from within that mess, taking to himself, for us, the worst life could do: betrayal and mortality:

> It's God they ought to crucify instead of you and me,
> I said to the carpenter a'hanging on the tree.[4]

All this can sometimes feel a bit 'out there' – great for discussion groups after midnight, but what of that 'dailyness' I was speaking of earlier? And that's the most extraordinary thing of all, as Paul's letter punches home. In the end it's about a God intensely involved in our everyday living and loving and struggling, its darkness and light. A God who when we cry out to him doesn't necessarily change the circumstances we're agonizing over – at all; *but transforms the way we experience them.* A God to whom each of us is so infinitely precious that not a tear we shed nor a joy we shout is unknown to him, and it all matters to him. A God who intervened in our disconnectedness to bridge the intolerable gap between our creativity and our destructiveness: not with endless rules with how to placate him, but with a Person, who suggested only two rules were necessary: love God with everything you've got, and love those around you as much as yourself. And when, hanging on to that Person, we begin to follow that road, we somehow find our connectedness with each other becomes real to us; and with the wheeling stars too, and the twitter of birds from that nest over there.

'This my God . . .', said Stewart Henderson:

> It is He Whom I will meet . . .
> and I will sink my face into the wonder of His glorylove
> and I will watch as planets converse with sparrows . . .'[5]

---

[4] Carter, S., *It was a Friday Morning*. Stainer and Bell, London, 1960. Extracts of the text of 'It was on a Friday morning (Friday Morning)' by Sydney Carter (1915–2004) © 1960 Stainer & Bell Ltd, 23 Gruneisen Road, London N3 1DZ, England <www.stainer.co.uk>. Used by permission.

[5] Henderson, S., 'The Last Enemy', published in *Assembled in Britain*. Marshall Pickering, London, 1986, p. 70; reproduced with permission. The full poem appears on p. 140.

For all things are reconciled in God, things on earth and things in heaven, by the peace made through Christ's living and loving and dying and living and loving. And so the chains fall. We are free from bondage. In the here and now, yes, though often it doesn't feel like it; the bruises of the chains have marked us. But in the for ever that lies beyond, we find he is Lord of our 'futures' as well as our 'now', and our ultimate freedom will only be experienced when, in his immediate and seen presence, we marvel at being part of unquenchable life, transformed as we were created to be. R. S. Thomas describes it:

> It's a long way off but inside it
> There are quite different things going on:
> Festivals at which the poor man
> Is king and the consumptive is
> Healed; mirrors in which the blind look
> At themselves and love looks at them
> Back; and industry is for mending
> The bent bones and the minds fractured
> By life. It's a long way off, but to get
> There takes no time and admission
> Is free, if you will purge yourself
> Of desire, and present yourself with
> Your need only and the simple offering
> Of your faith, green as a leaf.[6]

'[S]o as to present you holy and blameless and irreproachable before him' (Colossians 1.22b).

Thanks be to God. Amen,

---

[6] Thomas, R. S., 'The Kingdom' in *Selected Poems*. Penguin Books, London, 2003, p. 91. Permission to reproduce sought.

Song

I scan you on the figured page
in tales of every distant age
and chant you in a holy song
but yet I hear, I see you wrong

I am so small
you are so all

and I would scent you in a flower
that flares and fails from hour to hour
and count your liberality
in berries bright upon the tree

but they are small
and you are all

or might I feel you in the sky
your cloudwind lifts my soul so high
or might I taste you in the spring
new-risen, cleanly carolling

I am so small
you are so all

but narrow is my inward sight
I do not spell your meanings right
and guttering my outward gaze
I do not steady trace your ways

my steps are small
to map your all

then break me wide your raging word
in flintstruck light from darkness stirred
and break me wide your dancing love
that soars the hawk, that swoops the dove

I am so small
you are so all in all.

'The Last Enemy'

And He Who each day
reveals a new masterpiece of sky
and Whose joy
can be seen in the eyelash of a child
Who when He hears of our smug indifference
can whisper an ocean into lashing fury
and talk tigers into padding roars
This my God
Whose breath is in the wings of eagles
Whose power is etched in the crags of mountains
It is He Whom I will meet
in Whose Presence I will find tulips and clouds
kneeling martyrs and trees
the whole vast praising of His endless creation
And He will grant the uniqueness
that eluded me in my earthly bartering with Satan
That day when He will erase the painful gasps of my ego
and I will sink my face into the wonder of His glorylove
and I will watch planets converse with sparrows
On that day
when death is finally dead

10

From tricky text to lifestyle change: the debate about application

DAVID DAY

The concept of a tricky text intrigues me – texts whose implications for Christian living are elusive or just plain baffling. Many seem offensive, shocking, immoral, out of tune with our taken-for-granted world, or just weird. These we call the tricky ones. But, as I reflect further, I wonder if there are any biblical texts that are not tricky in some sense.

I make this suggestion because all biblical texts raise the question: 'Is there a sure way of reading contemporary significance out of an old book?' As ideas travel from Then to Now, they need to be processed. In the engaging words of Ernest Best,

> The remoteness of the words . . . may compel us to use some device or trick to unlock the meaning . . . We may look on Scripture as a deep freeze. When we need a sermon we go and bring out a text and after a suitable period of defrosting and cooking our meal is ready.[1]

This gap between text and sermon raises a related question: how can ancient words provoke action in modern hearers? I remember a conversation with an experienced pastor from the Far East. He confided that he had preached for nine years to the same congregation and was not aware of any great change in attitude or

---

[1] Best, E., *From Text to Sermon: Responsible Use of the New Testament in Preaching*. T. & T. Clark, Edinburgh, 1988, p. 55.

behaviour in his flock. Did I have any advice to give, he wondered. In the same vein a layman commented: 'After 50 years of going to church I suddenly realized it was all nonsense. I heard a 45-minute sermon on Paul's meeting with Festus – from every angle. I came away with an excellent understanding of a meeting that took place 2,000 years ago. But no better equipped in how to help the un-believing members of my family to find faith.'

This chapter explores issues raised by these comments. They concern not just tricky texts but every text; not just biblical truth but contemporary significance; not just dutiful hearing but lifestyle change.

The Application Emphasis

We are not short of advice if we are looking for the 'device or trick' that, after defrosting, will allow us to cook nourishing meals. Much of the 'hermeneutics industry' has focused on just this question. Homileticians have wrestled with the bridge model of interpreta-tion, with a variety of sermon structures, with narrative preaching, with moves and loops and types, as well as with time-honoured recipes like allegorization, spiritualization and illuminating an-achronisms. But what will effect change? How is the ancient text to work its magic? I do not wish to add to the literature on herme-neutics. What interests me is a current emphasis that addresses itself squarely to the issue of changing lives.

I shall refer to this movement as 'the Application Emphasis'. I am unsure whether it is yet influential enough to be deemed a movement; but it is not difficult to find books and articles that, together, may be said to constitute a distinctive emphasis.[2] Of course designing sermons that will change lives has been a concern of preachers from the very beginning. On the day of Pentecost

---

[2] Characteristic aspects of this movement are set out in Stanley, A. and Jones, L., *Communicating for a Change*. Multnomah, Portland, OR, 2006. See also York, H. and Blue, S., 'Is application necessary in the expository sermon?, *Southern Baptist Journal of Theology* 3.2 (Summer 1999), pp. 70–84.

Peter was not distressed to hear his congregation ask, 'What shall we do . . . to be saved?' But the recent renewed interest in life-change as an aim, and application as a means to achieving that aim, is worth examination. What are the characteristic marks of this emphasis?

1

The Application Emphasis sits most comfortably within the tradition of expository preaching. God wishes to communicate with humanity and has put the Scriptures at the centre of that communicative thrust. The Bible is therefore at the heart of any preaching worth its name. But the Scriptures are part of an ancient world. The Bible becomes a word from God to the individual or the community only in so far as the sermon makes relevant connections between the ancient text and the modern world. The time-honoured structure of exegesis, explanation (or exposition) and application is a sound one, but application must be given its proper weight. Preaching that concentrates solely on explaining the biblical text in its context is not proper or effective preaching. It is a lecture. Aiming to teach congregations the Bible is not preaching; it is information transfer. All this leads to the conclusion that a substantial proportion of the sermon must be devoted to application. It is not to be reduced to a few remarks tacked on at the end. One prominent representative of this position even advocates reducing the exposition to one point only. Congregations will forget four points before they reach the door, so preachers who are concerned about change will spend their energies isolating the one point and then ruthlessly eliminating everything else they might want to say.

2

The term 'application' assumes that hearers will not automatically connect the Word of God to their personal lives. Congregations need to be helped to see how a truth, an insight or a command might make a difference to their understanding or behaviour. This aim is widely recognized as a stage in sermon construction that it is easy to ignore or sideline. Characteristically, application will deal with the question 'So what? Why is this passage important to me?' and will portray various life situations within the congregation in order to explore how the 'one point' or 'main idea' plays out. It will necessarily take the form of individualized examples, tailored to the lives of recognizable types. This will often involve generalizing the biblical truth so that the application of it may speak to a wide range of people. The language will be concrete and specific, making use of examples, life-contexts, instances, and focusing on 'felt needs'. By such methods a preacher aims to respond to the problem set out by Jonathan Leeman in a fictional letter to a preacher:

> I'm trying really hard to be a better husband, and worker, and citizen, and parent, and to wear all the other hats I have to wear . . . I mean, Greek verb tenses and Old Testament typological structures are sort of interesting to me . . . Yet I'm trying to figure out what those things have to do with how I go to work on Monday, and how I speak to my little girl, and what I do with my money. These are the decisions that face me as soon as I walk out of your building.[3]

3

The third aspect of the application movement tries to ensure that the thrust of the sermon is carried forward into action. The process has been summarized as 'What?'; 'So what?'; 'Now what?' The stress on change highlights the saying, 'The Bible was not written to satisfy your curiosity; it was written to transform your life.' Danny Akin elaborates this distinctive emphasis:

> Aim for specific action on the part of your people. Fuzzy thinking is deadly to any aspect of a sermon, especially

---

[3] Leeman, J., 'Maybe I do want topical preaching?' *9 Marks* (21 August 2014).

in the portions dealing with the application of the biblical text . . . we must remember we are preaching to sheep. Sheep need very specific and particular guidance and direction. We must not assume they understand on their own . . . We cannot hope our people will 'fill in the blanks' of sermon application. Practical steps that are challenging but obtainable by God's grace and Christ's strength are our goal.[4]

This goal is supported by various homiletical strategies: clear delineation of what is involved, bolstered by exhortation; motivational rhetoric that links action with a vision of what God has done for us in Christ; stories of others who embody the life change that is being commended; specific and achievable targets set within a time frame; setting out a vision of how the world might look if the church, as individuals and as a community, chose to put the sermon into practice; a memorable slogan that reiterates the main point and will embody the message.

The thrust of the Application Emphasis is well summarized by Andy Stanley:

Bottom line: application – application makes all the difference. Bottom line: doing is what makes the difference – not believing, not hearing, not listening, not note taking, not elbow poking, not, yeah, yeah, yeah, I ought to – doing is what makes all the difference.[5]

Some strengths of the Application Emphasis

My outline of the main aspects of the Application Emphasis may be something of a caricature. It would be unfair not to mention that it has been subject to substantial self-criticism even by those who are broadly in sympathy with the approach. But caricatures have their uses. This one may sharpen up some of the defects of

---

[4] Akin, D., 'Sermon application: how does it work?', *Preaching* (1 September 2011).
[5] Stanley, A., 'Application is everything', *Sermon Central* (May 2013).

conventional preaching or draw attention to those aspects that go unnoticed or marginalized.

1 The Application Emphasis tends to reinstate the ministry of the Word. It assumes that God has something he wishes to say, and is thus a corrective against preaching that buries itself in the biblical text and never comes out. Such preaching risks treating the Bible as an historical relic and turning the sermon into a lecture or a commentary. It is equally opposed to sermons that sit lightly to the text, using it as a jumping-off point for a few personal reflections or as a pretext for social commentary.

2 Specific application proclaims that sermons are clearly relevant to the lives people lead outside the church. They deal with the practical and specific details of life and engage the whole person. Haddon Robinson observes the difference between this emphasis within preaching and the conventional sermon. 'Today, what's prevalent is specific application. In the past, the application would have been more general – to trust God and give him glory. Today, preaching deals with how to have a happy marriage, how to bring up your children, how to deal with stress.'[6]

3 The emphasis on life-change gives preaching a new dignity. Sermons have a point; they do something. They intend 'that Christ should be formed' in the congregation. This high view of preaching matches that expounded by Walter Brueggemann:

> We undertake theatre that is potentially life-changing. This is the meeting. This is where the transformation action takes place. This is not talk about some other meeting somewhere else. This dramatic moment intends that folk should go away changed, perhaps made whole, perhaps savaged.'[7]

---

[6] Robinson, H, 'The Heresy of Application', *Preaching Today* (2015).

[7] Brueggemann, W., *The Bible and Post-Modern Imagination: Texts Under Negotiation*. SCM Press, London, 1993, p. 24.

Questions for the Application Emphasis

The focus on application has some value for the preacher but it is clearly not the final word. In this last section I want to raise three questions relevant to the discussion.

1 From then to now or now to then?

The conventional move in application has been from biblical passage to contemporary implication. What might happen if that movement were reversed? Richard Briggs argues that immersing ourselves in the scriptural text could be seen as enriching our experience. He suggests that 'the kinds of issues and questions that will end up emphasized and probed will be both theologically important and also of relevance to today's differently shaped issues and questions'.[8] In the search for relevant application, perhaps it is not always a good thing to let today's agenda predetermine what counts as constructive engagement with the Bible. He observes that 'Scripture in its wonderful irrelevance is frequently in the business of changing the subject.' The biblical text may set a new agenda, redefining the nature of reality, bringing other insights to the fore and pushing our ideas of what makes for reality and relevance into the shadows.

Much the same point is made by Walter Brueggemann. He pictures a congregation settling down to listen to a sermon. Perhaps they are comfortably at home in 'old liturgical habits', or 'a thin suburban morality of competence or success', or 'the orthodoxy of liberal social causes'. What the preacher brings is 'an old, angular text', clearly out of date and irrelevant. However, if the preacher does not lose his or her nerve, the presumed world with which the congregation began is contradicted by the proposed world of the Bible. The movement back into the text, inhabiting its world, shows me 'texts that do not fit, dreams that expose my skewed

---

[8] Briggs, R., 'These are the days of Elijah: the hermeneutical move from applying the text to living in its world', *Journal of Theological Interpretation* 8.2 (2014), p. 173.

ego-structure and invite me to run beyond myself, that is to say, my old-self'.[9]

This experience is not unlike what occurs when going to the theatre or cinema or reading a good novel. We need not hurry out of the play, film or book in order to draw parallels with our own situation. As we identify with the fictional characters we learn about ourselves. Messages are communicated, but we are only half-aware of them. That does not mean that we are not affected, often profoundly, by what we see or read. Rather it cautions us not to rush to identify detailed ways in which the text might apply to our life situation.

2 Word of exhortation or imaginative vision?

The Application Emphasis works best with material that is obviously life-centred and deals with behaviour and ethics. However, it is easy to domesticate a sermon that stays in this mode, with the result that somewhere the power of the poetry and the grandeur of the vision are lost. The application to a sermon on 'Mary said "Yes" to God' ought to come out as more than 'You ought to contribute to the fund for the renovation of the side chapel roof'.

This is not to say that preaching will never exhort, but it is not the only way of using words. The roles played by powerful images or metaphors or a vision of truth that stirs the emotions are equally critical. 'Metaphors rearrange the furniture of the mind.' The kind of preaching that will suit this task has been characterized by Kate Bruce as 'lyrical preaching'. The lyrical voice majors on analogy, metaphor and simile, aims that the hearers should 'see through their ears' and works through employing all the functions of the imagination.[10] Seeing the world differently creates a desire to live in it differently.

---

[9] Brueggemann, *The Bible and Post-Modern Imagination*, p. 23.

[10] Bruce, K., *Igniting the Heart: Preaching and Imagination*. SCM Press, London, 2015, pp. 55–84.

For this reason it is important for preachers to offer their hearers a vision of Christ that will touch the emotions and the will as well as instructing the mind. Application in the strict sense is not necessary. Let the imagination be caught by a powerful vision of Jesus, and the implications of that vision will look after themselves. Lyrical preaching aims to bring him off the page.

In a similar way sermons can also effect change by shaping people's views of themselves. It is a theme that runs through the epistles: 'Once you were . . . now you are'; 'you are a royal priesthood', 'children of light', 'a new creation'. These descriptions are intended to catch the imagination, and by touching the heart they constitute an enormously powerful catalyst for change. But, again, the vision works by showing hearers who they are in Christ, and again, strict application is not essential.

3 All alone or with the body of Christ?

The Application Emphasis, as we have seen, stresses change as the ultimate goal of preaching. However, its depiction of the process seems to present the preacher's task as an essentially solitary one. The preacher works on the text, imagines the specific life situations of the hearers, decides on the practical implications of the main idea of the passage and devises methods of speaking persuasively into individual contexts.

Against this view, it has been often pointed out that God's purpose in redemption was to create a new humanity via a new community. Are there ways in which the event of preaching can work through the body of Christ? Groups like Alcoholics Anonymous and Weight Watchers exemplify the value of the group. Members commit themselves to a common task, articulating their individual stories, supporting one another in the process of changing behaviour, protecting one another from the pressure to slip back and helping to heal the wounds of failure. Is it possible that Christians might do some of that in church? Paul exhorts the church at Colossae to let 'the word of Christ dwell in you richly'

(Colossians 3.16) – as so often, the pronoun is in the plural. Yet much preaching presupposes an individual, who speaks, talking to a group of listeners, who are silent.

More attention needs to be given to the role of the community in changing lives. It is possible for the congregation to be involved in sermon preparation, in the delivery of the sermon – café church and other fresh expressions – and in responding to the sermon.[11] Undergirding these activities is the assumption that the congregation expects to be involved and comes ready and *able* to listen. William Willimon says firmly: 'Preaching is dependent on a listening community and how well it has learned to hear scripture preached as scripture . . . as that master story that subsumes and thereby transforms all other stories!' 'Faithful preaching is frighteningly dependent on faithful listening.'[12] We spend little time on helping congregations to hear sermons.

The Application Emphasis can often seem over-confident, dogmatic, even patronizing. Yet it provokes us to think more carefully about the claims we unthinkingly make about preaching: how the Bible speaks into contemporary life, what constitutes responsible application, and how serious we are about transformation. It is only natural for us to critique what may seem to be no more than the latest fad, but we should also be open to listening to it. We have much to learn from the resulting dialogue.

---

[11] See for example, McClure, J. S., *The Roundtable Pulpit*. Abingdon, Nashville, TN, 1995; Tubbs Tisdale, L., *Preaching as Local Theology and Folk Art*. Fortress Press, Minneapolis, MN, 1997; Van Harn, R. E., *Pew Rights*. Eerdmans, Grand Rapids, MI, 1992; Thomson, J., *Is the Sermon a Sacred Cow?* Grove Books, Cambridge, 1996; Stratford, T., *Interactive Preaching*. Grove Books, Cambridge, 1998.
[12] Willimon, W. H. and Hauerwas, S., *Preaching to Strangers*. Westminster John Knox Press, Louisville, KY, 1992, pp. 135–8.

Afterword

JAMIE HARRISON

The Dean Emeritus of Durham, Michael Sadgrove, is no lover of sloppy sermons, nor of those that sit loose to text or context. Michael calls preaching a 'public *liturgical* act'.[1] He has no time for sermons that go on too long, ignore the text, play to the gallery, moralize, lack shape or direction, or fall into cliché. His top deadly sin for the preacher, however, is to be boring![2]

In the book *Christ in a Choppy Box*, where a choppy box is the trough from which pit ponies in the North East feed (and hence a type of manger), we find some of his sermons. I can vouch for Michael's wit and wisdom, as he becomes a player in the 'holy theatre' of the liturgy, in which 'numinous reality can be felt and touched'. His choppy box is indeed a place from which to gain sustenance, and not of the straw variety!

Michael is no fan of the free-standing sermon, 'an isolated activity' that fails to engage with the flow of the liturgy (or worship service). He sees the preacher as an artist, the sermon as art form. Yet there are works of art that proudly, and provocatively, challenge on their own terms. They have the power to shock: unrepentant prisms and mirrors. In this sense, the tricky text, the difficult passage, the unsavoury verse, act as irritants, to unsettle and to provoke. Is such a preached text consistent with, or in discontinuity with, the worship of which it forms a part? Can such a sermon work to form a pearl out of the friction between the sermon content and the liturgical focus? But perhaps I am

---

[1] Sadgrove, M. C., *Christ in a Choppy Box: Sermons from North East England*, ed. Harrison, C. Sacristy Press, Durham, 2015, p. 11.

[2] Sadgrove, *Christ in a Choppy Box*, pp. 12, 23–4.

being unfair, for Michael is not one to ignore the place and purpose of a given text. Neither is David Day, to whom this book is
dedicated.

Wrestling with the Word

David Day's approach to preaching, embodying the central tenet
of this book, is to take the whole of Scripture seriously, and not
to be afraid to grapple with its most difficult texts in public. To
voice such texts exposes the preacher to criticism and complaint,
exposing a vulnerability that many would wish to avoid. In his
writing, teaching and preaching, David has inspired countless students, ordinands, clergy, lay preachers and Readers in the Church
of England to take risks and to allow the Scriptures to speak.

David writes that the need 'to do justice to the whole passage
is often very difficult, because we find it easier to leave out those
verses which don't fit'.[3] He gives an example of some proposed
sermons on Mark's account of the healing of a leper (Mark
1.40–45). One embryonic sermon wanted to explore Jesus' healing
ministry in general, another to avoid any reference to healing at
all. These offerings left David uneasy, as both 'intended to gloss
over or ignore the surprising or awkward bits of the story'.

Ever the supportive mentor, David writes of sharing the temptation not to notice the awkward verse, or of being content for a
reading to be cut just before the difficult point is reached.

My main point here is that if we ignore parts of the passage,
or use it as a pretext for some message of our own, we
devalue the word which we have been given. It is not allowed
to speak in its own, distinctive tone. The Bible becomes,
in Craddocks's phrase, 'wall-paper or background music'.
However tricky the passage, we are called to *wrestle with it*.[4]

---

[3] Day, D. V., *A Preaching Workbook*. SPCK, London, 1998, p. 18.
[4] Day, *A Preaching Workbook*, pp. 19–20 (my italics).

Elsewhere, David highlights Karl Barth's maxim that 'Preachers must love their congregations'.[5] He reflects that this is not always easy, not least when 'the sermon is just a chore . . . and we don't much like the people we preach to'. But he goes on to express his own understanding of the calling of a preacher, words with which it seems fitting to conclude this Afterword:

> In all this I am not trying desperately to communicate passion, stillness and love. To attempt to do so would be an artificial exercise and one which would call my integrity into question. I pursue these qualities and persevere in the quest in the faith that this is what a preacher should be like. I don't focus on myself in order that I should be an effective speaker of sermons. I concentrate on myself in the presence of God because that is what I ought to do. It is the heart of my devotion, my identity and my discipleship. Yet, as I seek God's face, I trust that he will so change me that, without my conscious effort, something of that renewed person will be caught and sensed by those to whom I speak.[6]

---

[5] Barth, K., *Homiletics*, trans. Bromily, G. W. and Daniels, D. E. Westminster John Knox Press, Louisville, KY, 1991, p. 84.

[6] Day, D. V., *Embodying the Word: A Preacher's Guide*. SPCK, London, 2005, p. 18.

Appendix
David Day – a life well preached

JAMIE HARRISON

David Day was born and bred in Tottenham, establishing a con-
nection that has been maintained by his irrational but dogged
devotion to Tottenham Hotspur FC. He read Classics at Queen Mary
College, University of London, and taught Latin, Greek and Religious
Education at secondary schools in North London and Nottingham.
After teaching for 15 years, he moved into higher education, first
as a Lecturer in Theology at Bishop Lonsdale College of Education
and then as Senior Lecturer in Education in the Durham University
School of Education. During this period he obtained Master's
degrees in both Education and Theology. In 1992 he was appointed Principal of St John's College with Cranmer Hall, Durham
University, a post he held until his retirement in 1999. While at
St John's he established the Centre for Christian Communication and taught preaching and communication to Anglican and
Methodist ordinands. Since retirement, he continues to contribute
to courses on preaching at Master's level, and to in-service training
for ministers, both lay and ordained.

David was first licensed as a Reader in the Church of England
in 1963, exercising an active ministry at St Cuthbert Chitt's Hill,
then Christ Church Chilwell, and finally at St Nicholas Durham.
In 1999 he was ordained deacon, and priested in 2000. He now
serves as Honorary Curate at St Nicholas Durham, his spiritual
home for 37 years.

David has broadcast many times on BBC Radio 2's *Pause for
Thought* and was Series Preacher for BBC television's *Christmas*

is Coming! He served on the Durham Commission on Religious Education, the Council of the College of Preachers, and the Management Committee of the North of England Institute for Christian Education. For many years he chaired the Durham County Council Standing Advisory Council on Religious education. He has written a number of school textbooks, a study of teenage faith, articles on values in Education, two books on preaching and is joint editor of a *Reader on Preaching*. He was also author of *Pearl Beyond Price* – the Archbishop of Canterbury's Lent book for 2002. What holds this disparate collection together is a concern for communicating the Christian faith in contemporary language. He is passionate about encouraging young preachers to test their call and learn their craft.

In March 2016, David was given the Lanfranc Award for Education and Scholarship by the Archbishop of Canterbury. This was for his 'contribution to Christian education and preaching'.

He is married to Rosemary, has three children and nine grandchildren, probably (he says) watches too much television, loves opera, Italy and films with subtitles, and enjoys fantasy football.

Select publications

This Jesus. Inter-Varsity Press, Leicester, 1979.

'Agreeing to Differ: the logic of pluralism' in Coffield, F. and Goodings, R. (eds), *Sacred Cows in Education: Essays in Reassessment.* Edinburgh University Press, Durham, 1983, pp. 77–90.

'God's People: the Church' in *A Faith for Life*. Lion Publishing, Tring, 1985.

Jeremiah: Speaking for God in a Time of Crisis. Inter-Varsity Press, Leicester, 1987.

  (trans) *Jérémie: Témoin de Dieu en un temps de crise.* Grâce et Vérité, Mulhouse, 1992.

  (trans) *Jeremias: Portavoz de Dios entiempos de crisis.* Publicaciones-Andamio, Barcelona, 2002.

It's Dark Inside. Lion Publishing, Tring, 1988.

(trans) *Kde se to v nasbere?* Nakladatelstvi Portal, Praha, 1994.

Why Don't You Grow Up? Lion Publishing, Tring, 1988.

(trans) *Hvorforbliver du ikkevoksen?*, Horsens, Alokke, 1990.

What's So Special? Lion Publishing, Tring, 1989.

(trans) *Proc NebytDospely?* Nakladatelstvi Portal, Praha, 1994.

Down to Earth: The Environment and How We Live In It (with McPartland, M.). Lion Publishing, Tring, 1990.

Teenage Beliefs (with May, P. R.). Lion Publishing, Oxford, 1991.

Weekly Theme Features (with Carey, G.) in *A Year with the Bible.* Lion Publishing, Oxford, 1991.

The Contours of Christian Education (ed. with Astley, J.). McCrimmons, Great Wakering, Essex, 1992.

'Apples of Gold: the role of proverbial wisdom in Christian education', in Day, D. V. and Astley, J. (eds), *The Contours of Christian Education.* McCrimmons, Great Wakering, Essex, 1992, pp. 162–76.

'Godliness and Good Learning: the role of the secondary school in the spiritual development of adolescent Christians', in Day, D. V. and Astley, J. (eds), *The Contours of Christian Education.* McCrimmons, Great Wakering, Essex, 1992, pp. 230–44.

'Empathy in Education', in Ashton, E. and Watson, B. (eds), *Society in Conflict: The Value of Education, Aspects of Education, Journal of the Institute of Education* 51. University of Hull (1994), pp. 90–6.

'Modell-Lehrpläne fur den Religionsunterricht: die jüngste Entwicklung in Grossbritannien', *Jahrbuch der Religionspädagogik.* Band 11 (1994), pp. 167–74.

'The Ministry of Laity', in Yeats, C. (ed.), *Has Keele Failed? Reform in the Church of England.* Hodder & Stoughton, London, 1995, pp. 104–16.

Beyond the Here and Now (with Astley, J.). Lion Publishing, Oxford, 1996.

'Exodus 3:14–17 Called by God to teach' (an address given to the Association of Christian Teachers), *Act Now* 42 (Summer 1997), pp. 5–8.

'Preaching the Epistles', *Anvil* 14: 4 (1997), pp. 273–82.

Die Leichte Unverständlichkeit des Seins. OnckenVerlag, Wuppertal und Kassel, 1998.

A Preaching Workbook. SPCK, London, 1998.

'Cuthbert as a Model Preacher', in Burton, L. and Whitehead, A. (eds) *Christ is the Morning Star*. Lindisfarne Books, Dublin, 1999, pp. 71–90.

'The Lenten Preacher', *The Journal of the College of Preachers* (January 1999), pp. 29–38.

Pearl Beyond Price: The Attractive Jesus; The Archbishop of Canterbury's Lent Book 2002. Zondervan, Harrow, UK and Grand Rapids, MI, 2001.

Christ our Life: Colossians (Emmaus Bible Resources). Church House Publishing, London, 2003.

Embodying the Word: A Preacher's Guide. SPCK, London, 2005.

A Reader on Preaching: Making Connections (ed. with Astley, J. and Francis, L.). Ashgate, Aldershot, 2005.

Select bibliography

Adam, P., *Speaking God's Words: A Practical Theology of Preaching*. Regent College Publishing, Vancouver, BC, 1996.

Baker, J., *Transforming Preaching: Communicating God's Word in a Postmodern World*. Grove Books, Cambridge, 2009.

Barrett, C. K., *The Gospel According to St John: An Introduction with Commentary and Notes on the Greek Text*. 2nd edn, SPCK, London, 1978.

Barth, K., *Homiletics*, trans. Bromily, G. W. and Daniels, D. E. Westminster John Knox Press, Louisville, KY, 1991.

Best, E., *From Text to Sermon: Responsible Use of the New Testament in Preaching*. T. & T. Clark, Edinburgh, 1988.

Bolz-Weber, N., *Accidental Saints: Finding God in All the Wrong People*. Canterbury Press, Norwich, 2015.

Briggs, R. S., *Fairer Sex: Spiritual Readings of Four Old Testament Passages about Men and Women*. Grove Books, Cambridge, 2015.

Bruce, K., *Igniting the Heart: Preaching and Imagination*. SCM Press, London, 2015.

Brueggemann, W., *Finally Comes the Poet: Daring Speech for Proclamation*. Fortress Press, Minneapolis, MN, 1989.

Brueggemann, W., *The Bible and Post-modern Imagination: Texts under Negotiation*. SCM Press, London, 1993.

Buechner, F., *Telling Secrets*. HarperOne, New York, 1991.

Buttrick, D., *Homiletic*. SCM Press, London, 1987.

Coggan, D., *On Preaching*. SPCK, London, 1978.

Craddock, F. B., *Preaching*. Abingdon, Nashville, TN, 1985.

Hare, D. R. A., *Matthew: Interpretation – A Bible Commentary for Teaching and Preaching*. John Knox Press, Louisville, KY, 1993.

Holden, A. and Holden, B. (eds), *Poems that Make Grown Men Cry: 100 Men on the Words that Move Them*. Simon & Schuster, New York, 2014.

James, C. C., *When Life and Belief Collide*. Zondervan, Grand Rapids, MI, 2002.

McClure, J. S., *The Roundtable Pulpit*. Abingdon, Nashville, TN, 1995.

Murray, S., *Post-Christendom, Church and Mission in a Strange New World*. Paternoster Press, Carlisle, 2004.

Norrington, D. C., *To Preach or Not to Preach*. Paternoster Press, Carlisle, 1996.

Northcutt, K. L., *Kindling Desire for God: Preaching as Spiritual Direction*. Fortress Press, Minneapolis, MN, 2009.

Pagitt, D., *Preaching Re-imagined: The Role of the Sermon in Communities of Faith*. Zondervan, Grand Rapids, MI, 2005.

Pritchard, J. P., *How to Explain your Faith*. SPCK, London, 2006.

Quicke, M. J., *360 Degree Preaching*. Baker Academic, Grand Rapids, MI, 2003.

Runia, K., *The Sermon Under Attack*. Paternoster Press, Exeter, 1983.

Sadgrove, M. C., *Christ in a Choppy Box: Sermons from North East England*, ed. Harrison, C. Sacristy Press, Durham, 2015.

Schama, S., *Rembrandt's Eyes*. Penguin, London, 1999.

Schama, S., *The Embarrassment of Riches: An Interpretation of Dutch Culture in the Golden Age*. HarperPerennial, London, 2004.

Stanley, A. and Jones, L., *Communicating for a Change*. Multnomah, Portland, OR, 2006.

Stratford, T., *Interactive Preaching*. Grove Books, Cambridge, 1998.

Thomson, J., *Is the Sermon a Sacred Cow?* Grove Books, Cambridge, 1996.

Tubbs Tisdale, L., *Preaching as Local Theology and Folk Art*. Fortress Press, Minneapolis, MN, 1997.

Van Harn, R. E., *Pew Rights*. Eerdmans, Grand Rapids, MI, 1992.

Weiser, A., *The Psalms*. SCM Press, London, 1962.

Williams, R., *The Dwelling of the Light: Praying with the Icons of Christ*. Canterbury Press, Norwich, 2003.

Willimon, W. H. and Hauerwas, S., *Preaching to Strangers*. Westminster John Knox Press, Louisville, KY, 1992.

Did you know that SPCK is a registered charity?

As well as publishing great books by leading Christian authors, we also . . .

. . . **make assemblies meaningful and fun for over a million children** by running www.assemblies.org.uk, a popular website that provides free assembly scripts for teachers. For many children, school assembly is the only contact they have with Christian faith and culture, and the only time in their week for spiritual reflection.

. . . **help prisoners to become confident readers** with our easy-to-read stories. Poor literacy is a huge barrier to rehabilitation. Prisoners identify with the believable heroes of our gritty fiction. At the same time, questions at the end of each chapter help them to examine their choices from a moral perspective and to build their reading confidence.

. . . **support student ministers overseas in their training** through partnerships in the Global South.

Please support these great schemes: visit www.spck.org.uk/support-us to find out more.